MORE THAN 70 EXPERTS ON THE
SUBJECT OF TURNING 70

THINGS TO DO
WHEN YOU TURN 70

Edited by Ronnie Sellers

Commissioning Editor Mark Evan Chimsky

Associate Project Editor Renee Rooks Cooley

SELLERS
PUBLISHING

Published by Sellers Publishing, Inc.

Copyright © 2013 Sellers Publishing, Inc.
All rights reserved.

Sellers Publishing, Inc.
161 John Roberts Road, South Portland, Maine 04106
Visit our Web site: www.sellerspublishing.com • E-mail: rsp@rsvp.com

Design by Faceout Studio

ISBN 13: 978-1-4162-0915-7
e-ISBN: 978-1-4162-0952-2
Library of Congress Control Number: 2013931257

The ideas and suggestions in this book are not intended as
a substitute for the medical advice of your trained health
professional. All matters regarding your health require medical
supervision. Where appropriate, consult your physician before
adopting the suggestions in this book, as well as about any
condition that may require diagnosis or medical attention.
The publisher disclaims any liability arising directly or
indirectly from the use of the book.

Printed in the United States of America.

Credits: page 303

CONTENTS

PART 2
Keeping Active and Caring for Your Body

PART 3
Nurturing Your Soul

INTRODUCTION

Most of us spend a great deal of time during the course of our lives looking for answers to the BIG questions. The amount of time we dedicate to this tends to increase the closer we get to the back door. Approaching, or celebrating, one's 70th birthday tends to be a powerful motivator for even the most die-hard procrastinator (like me) to take stock and start trying to get some of these questions answered. If you're reading this book, you're probably coming up on the 70-mile marker (or have recently passed it) and in the market for some guidance about what to do with the rest of your life. You came to the right place.

I don't know for certain, but I have a hunch the editors had an ulterior motive when they asked me to write the introduction for this book about turning 70. They knew that if I accepted the assignment I'd have to read all the insightful, humorous, informative essays it contains. They know me pretty well . . . well enough to know it won't be long before I turn 70. They'd never admit it, but I suspect they think I'm in urgent need of some good advice about how to "get a life."

This is ironic, because when I was a young man I knew everything there was to know about life. I was the smartest, most perceptive and spiritually aware person I knew. Everyone I came into contact with knew this, primarily because I made sure I told them. I told them because I was also the most generous and altruistic person I knew. I had a moral obligation to share my wisdom.

For example, I have vivid memories of luncheons with my 70-year-old grandfather during which I imparted my wisdom to him. This was a man who was born on a farm in North Carolina, was forced to leave school in the eighth grade to work in the fields, and then still managed to start a retail business in Philadelphia, operate it for 40 years, and become a pillar of the community. It was a measure of my brilliance, I remember thinking to myself, that someone my age could give such valuable and introspective advice to a man who'd encountered, and overcome, so many challenges.

I had no doubt that he was deeply grateful for the wisdom I bestowed upon him — so grateful, in fact, that he was unable to find the words to express his appreciation adequately. So he would just sit there in silence with his hands folded in his lap, gaze into my eyes, and smile fondly as he took it all in.

Much to my surprise, as time went on, things began to change. I grew dumber with age. I began to realize that I didn't have all the answers. While this was disconcerting, it wasn't without its benefits. For one thing, it enabled me to have a few friends. I first became aware of this at work. When I was smarter, the break room seemed to empty out moments after I entered. As I became less sagacious, a few people would actually stay around long enough to talk with me. Eventually, my profundity decreased to the point where I actually got invited to a few parties.

Fast-forward to the year that my son turned 16. This was the point at which I hit bottom and became totally ignorant. I possessed absolutely no knowledge about anything that was in the least bit valuable or worth sharing. I knew this because my son told me so at least three times a day. Perhaps you have had children, too. If you have, then you've probably also been made aware of how totally stupid you are on at least a few occasions.

So you see, the ugly truth is that the editors were right. I really did need to read this book. I have read it, and I'm better off for it. It infused me with optimism about my prospects for my life at 70 and beyond. As Elaine Madsen advises at the beginning of her essay, "The first thing to do when you turn 70 is to plan on being 80." I'm now making that plan.

I found comfort in Dorian Mintzer's essay, "Turning 70!," in which she writes, "Although we can't control everything in life, there is certainly a lot we *can* control. Appreciate your own life, and the perspective and wisdom that you have gained from confronting life's challenges." This seems like good solid counsel to me. The older we get, the more vulnerable we feel. If we focus on the things we do have control over, we'll have less time to ponder and fret about life's uncertainties.

If I had to summarize what this book is about in one sentence, I'd say, "It's a book that inspires you to keep growing as you hit, and pass, your 70th year." Growth rarely happens without change. Bob Lowry explains in his essay that "about three years into my retirement I realized I was wasting the most precious of all gifts we are given: time. In a burst of energy — and with a fresh perspective — I began to experiment with new hobbies and interests." He and his wife downsized, simplified their lives, trained to become spiritual counselors, and spent six years helping people with emotional, physical, or medical problems. They changed, they gave, and they grew together.

Don't get me wrong: this book contains lots of practical advice as well. I found Vickie Dellaquila's advice about downsizing your home to be particularly useful (and relevant). "Remember that every item you own requires your time, energy, maintenance, and money." We all carry the hoarder gene, but Vickie explains how to keep your stuff from burying you alive.

What I found to be among the most piquant statements in the book came from none other than Mark Twain: "The seventieth birthday! It is the time of life when you arrive at a new and awful dignity; when you may throw aside the decent reserves which have oppressed you for a generation and stand unafraid and unabashed upon your seven-terraced summit and look down and teach — unrebuked." And so, to paraphrase Twain slightly, "A sound maxim is this: That we can't reach 70 by another man's road."

I think every contributor to this book would agree that we must each find our own path to 70. How wonderful of them to offer us the benefit of their experiences to guide us along our way!

Ronnie Sellers
July 2013

Part

BEING MINDFUL OF LIVING FULLY

I

Seventy: Go and Be Happy

by Nikki Giovanni

Nikki Giovanni is a world-renowned poet, writer, commentator, activist, and educator. Over the past 30 years, her outspokenness, in her writing and lectures, has brought the eyes of the world upon her. One of the most widely read American poets, she prides herself on being "a Black American, a daughter, a mother, a professor of English." Giovanni remains as determined and committed as ever to the fight for civil rights and equality. Always insisting on presenting the truth as she sees it, she has maintained a prominent place as a strong voice of the Black community. Her focus is on the individual, specifically on the power one has to make a difference in oneself and, thus, in the lives of others.

I'm not a fan of the idea of the "bucket" list. If you're going to do it, do it now. Even if you're just 69. Fall in love. With yourself. Again. Make beautiful meals. For yourself. Balance the orange carrots (sliced on the slope) with the thin, thin onions sautéed in butter. Broccoli steamed to just bright green. Chicken leg with skin on. (If you made it to 70 or even just 69, eat the skin! How long do you think you'll live anyway?) And an incredible Washington State red wine. Dessert? Sliced oranges sugared or blackberries in cream. And every now and then, just to remember the good old days, homemade fudge. Plan it. Cook it. Eat it. Enjoy it.

Fall in love with your skin. Again. Buy the very best bath salts you can afford. Nah, go into debt and get something way beyond your means, and bathe in it. Shea butter the angels themselves have whipped to gently rub all over. And definitely treat yourself to a great perfume. Even if you're not going to see anyone. Especially if you've lost your sense of smell. You'll know you're in the groove by the way the flowers are hanging their heads as you walk from bath to bedroom.

Find a really great radio station that plays real jazz . . . not that crappy "smooth" or awful "watercolory" stuff but music . . . Louis Armstrong; Ella Fitzgerald; Lady Day; Pres; The Divine One; Duke, but most assuredly *Live at Newport*; and The Count, most especially *The Atomic Basie*; Sweets; The Jazz Messengers; and please don't forget Mark Murphy.

You're 70. Or maybe only 69, so this is just a beginning. Fall in love. With someone. And don't play that silly game that says they have to fall in love back. Squeeze every ounce of what is good from the feeling and leave the future to folk who have mortgages to sign off on and term life to start paying. I'm saying this is your car. You drive it. If you get a passenger for part of the trip, good for you. If not, let the top down and hit the road. You were a good daughter/a good son/a good sister/a good brother/a good niece/a good nephew/a good worker/a good saver/a good investor/a good credit risk/a good every damn thing. Now Go and Be Happy.

2

Play's the Thing

by Daniel M. Klein

Daniel M. Klein is the coauthor, with Thomas Cathcart, of the international best-seller *Plato and a Platypus Walk into a Bar.* More recently, Klein wrote *Travels with Epicurus* (Penguin) about the philosophy of old age. A graduate of Harvard in philosophy, he has written comedy for television and mystery novels, in addition to books about philosophy.

Play's the thing wherein we'll capture the kingly pleasures of being old men. That is, if we can remember *how* to play. Somewhere in that ticklish period between childhood and geezerhood, we lose track of that fundamental delight: fooling around for no purpose other than the joy it yields to us.

In that middle period, we are so busy striving, so besot by ambition, that building sand castles on the beach or playing old songs on the accordion in the backyard are deemed a waste of time. What doth it profit a man in his prime to simply play? Nothing at all — except fun. Sure, we may have gone to the gym during that go-get-'em stage, but not for fun; we went with serious purpose: to lose weight, build stamina, and to stay young. But in our 70s, there is no percentage in trying to stay young for the simple reason that we're too old to stay young.

Again, in those middle years, we may have "played hard." But in that period of relentlessly measuring our success against others, the genuine play of childhood bit the dust. We may have played basketball or handball or golf, but in order to *win*. That is not authentic play; authentic play is pointless. In the end, "playing hard" sounds an awful lot like work. No fun in that.

But now, we geezers have the wonderful opportunity to get down on all fours and play for no reason other than the sheer hell of it.

A memory from my young adulthood is my personal inspiration: in 1961, I was in graduate school in Paris and feeling lonely in a late-adolescent, Parisian sort of way. I took moody walks, and on one of these I wandered through a stone archway that led into a park called the Arènes de Lutèce. In this nearly hidden spot, I came upon the remnants of the Romans' first-century outpost, complete with a mammoth amphitheater.

I climbed to the top of the gallery and sat. Below me, on the same ground where gladiators once played their lethal games, a group of six old Frenchmen were playing *boules*. What struck me immediately was the grace and decorum of these old guys: all wore jackets and ties; some sported berets; and their demeanor with one another was both genteel — a finely executed bowl was acknowledged with polite bows — and warmly familiar. They smiled and laughed frequently; they touched one another's backs and shoulders easily and often. But above all, this sextet of handsome, dignified old geezers played with gusto.

I found the spectacle deeply moving. The players' happiness floated up to me. Looking back now, I believe that much of the exhilaration I felt came from the fact that these were *old* guys, at the far end of life from where I sat, yet they were still reveling in the joy of being alive.

I fully understood what Plato meant when he stated that pure play has intimations of the divine. In a section of the *Laws*, he wrote: "Man is made God's plaything, and that is the best part of him. . . . Therefore every man and woman should live life accordingly, and play the noblest games. . . . What, then, is the right way of living? Life must be lived as play."

Nota bene, my fellow septuagenarians.

This essay is adapted by the author from his book *Travels with Epicurus*, published by Penguin and reprinted with permission.

3

On Aging and Turning 70

by Allan N. Schwartz, Ph.D., LCSW

Allan N. Schwartz, Ph.D., LCSW has been engaged in the practice of clinical social work and psychotherapy for more than 35 years. He has worked in the psychiatric departments of major hospitals in New York City, including the Geriatric Psychiatric Outpatient Clinic of the Bronx Municipal Hospital Center (Jacobi Medical Center), and also had an active private practice in Manhattan. He continues to see patients in Boulder, Colorado, incorporating technology into his practice through the use of online psychotherapy and real-time video. In addition, Dr. Schwartz writes articles on mental health for the Web site MentalHelp.net.

I am about to celebrate my 70th birthday. This has prompted me to pause and reflect about what it really means. While there is much information available on the positive aspects of aging, it is far outweighed by the negative. Most articles dwell on issues of illness, death, and grieving. Is this what aging is really about? Not necessarily. So, here are my observations about entering my eighth decade.

As I have aged, I've accumulated a wellspring of wisdom and experience that's made me a better psychotherapist. In working with young adults, I find it easier to relate to their situations because I've been there. I can even relate to their parents as they discuss coping with their adult children. I've learned the art of being very patient with my patients. I am better at communicating my knowledge and life experience to them. In fact, I have noticed that my thinking is much clearer than it used to be. My background and years of practice have also made me more self-confident, even in dealing with difficult cases.

The stereotype of people who are aging is that they become less flexible in their opinions and attitudes. Speaking for myself, it's become easier to admit to my mistakes when relating to family, friends, and patients. Despite the saying "you can't teach an old dog new tricks," this old dog is even more open to learning than when he was younger. Perhaps that's because I no longer worry that asking for help or seeking clarification will be perceived as a sign of weakness. Ego and pride are no longer associated with "not knowing."

Of course, the fact of death can't be overlooked. However, I question whether death enters our thoughts more at a later age than when we were younger. No one is safe from death. Tragedy and loss can and do occur throughout our life span. During my 70 years, I have witnessed the deaths of friends, family, and patients whose ages ranged from teens to the elderly. Some died in a gradual manner, as the result of disease, while others perished from sudden and unpredictable events, such as car accidents. In our youth-oriented society, it's easy to presume that the elderly spend their days dwelling on morbid thoughts, while younger people, who are busy living life, don't have time to be preoccupied with death. But becoming depressed over death can happen at any age. Getting older is not inherently sad, tragic, or the end of living.

Finally, I am much better able to live in and appreciate living in the moment. I feel much less pressure to be somewhere, to meet some deadline, and to attain some difficult goal. Maybe that is part of the solution to the stresses of living and aging: live mindfully, and don't be in such a hurry to get to the next place and the next task. In other words, the past is gone, the future may never be, but we have the present. Whatever your age, live fully in the moment!

This essay was adapted by the author from his article that appeared in MentalHelp.net.

4

What's the Point?

Ideas for a Satisfying and Meaningful Life in Your 70s

by Bill Roiter, Ed.D.

Bill Roiter, Ed.D., is a psychologist, executive coach, businessman, author, and consultant to people as they move beyond work. His book *Beyond Work: How Accomplished People Retire Successfully* (Wiley) won the bookstore owners' and librarians' Axiom Gold Medal as the best retirement book of 2009. He contributed essays to 65 *Things to Do When You Retire* and 65 *Things to Do When You Retire: Travel* (both published by Sellers Publishing). Also, Dr. Roiter is a clinical instructor at Harvard Medical School and a consultant to many organizations, including those in the financial, higher education, life sciences, retail, health care, and not-for-profit sectors, as well as other business areas.

I recently had a conversation with an accomplished 68-year-old man about his upcoming retirement. He was not happy; his life had been defined by his very satisfying professional career. "Now what?" he asked. "I loved the challenge of my work; it was win or lose, and I mostly won. The greater the challenge, the greater the satisfaction. I have a wonderful wife, two kids, a grandson, and some good friends. I enjoy them all, but where is the challenge, what is the point? The 70s really do seem like 'God's waiting room.' I am not looking forward to it; I'm already missing the past." Not everyone feels this way as they look to their 70s, but it is more frequent than you may think. So, how do we make these years the best they can be? Here are some ideas that may be of help:

1. **Seek satisfaction and meaning in your life.** As you continue to grow and change in your 70s, think about what will make your life satisfying and meaningful now that you may not be working. Satisfaction comes from doing what you enjoy, while meaning comes from doing what is important to you. What are the things you like to do, and what gives your life purpose?

2. **Are you continuing to move your life forward as you age, or are you now just getting old?** Aging continues to offer *opportunities* to rethink and

refocus on what's important. Getting old is more about the *barriers* we face due to loss of function. We can manage our own perceptions of these physical changes. However, if we let others define us as old and we accept their point of view, then we will be concentrating only on our limitations. If we accept and define ourselves as aging naturally, then we'll look for our opportunities.

3. **Act on what is satisfying and meaningful to you, the important things in life.** How are you doing? Your answer is a reflection of your sense of well-being. You can improve the quality of your life by looking at these four components:

    1) **Financial well-being.** How secure is your financial situation? Get as much financial-planning assistance as possible. There are great resources available on the Internet and in most communities. While it's good that rich people plan their finances, it is critical that the rest of us do so, too.

    2) **Physical well-being.** How informed are you about your current and future health? Manage your health and deal with any "wild card"

physical problems that arise. Be sure to find the best doctor you can afford, and ask questions so you understand your health needs and options.

3) **Social well-being**. Do you have people in your life you enjoy spending time with? Create a community of family and friends that is based on who you are rather than what you do.

4) **Personal well-being**. How confident are you that you are making the most of your life? The three categories above feed your sense of personal well-being, which is ultimately what it means to be successful in your 70s. Can you build your life around the knowledge of what's important to you?

Take some time to think about the goals and priorities that have meaning to you and how you want to reach them. If you have trouble with this, seek out trusted family, friends, and advisors to talk it over. Are you doing things that are consistent with your priorities? If not, can you begin to do so now?

5

Daring to Be 70

Elaine Madsen is an Emmy Award–winning documentary filmmaker, director, and published author. The Rhode Island International Film Festival honored her most recent documentary, I *Know a Woman Like That*, with its Helping Hand International Humanitarian Award. The film was produced by her daughter Virginia Madsen's Title IX Productions. Madsen is the author of *Crayola Can't Make These Colors . . . from the Palette of a Life in Verse* and the coauthor, with Douglass Stewart, of *The Texan and Dutch Gas: Kicking Off the European Energy Revolution*, both available online. She resides in California with her husband, Edward Carstens.

The first thing to do when you turn 70 is to plan on being 80. A valuable guide to fulfilling that plan is this quote from Edith Hamilton's book *The Greek Way*:

The Greeks believed happiness is the exercise of vital powers along lines of excellence in a life affording them scope.

According to Plato, a famous ancient Greek called Socrates said:

The life unexamined is not worth living.

So, upon arriving at 70, you must examine your life to discern:

What are your own vital powers? What are your personal lines of excellence? Within what scope can you exercise both?

When you've completed this personal inventory and have answered those questions about your life, you will find yourself. To quote a very wise friend of mine, Suzanne Adams:

This is a time to be fearless.

She continued:

To be flat-footed about it, there's only a certain amount of life you have left to lose!

So, dare to try something you've never done — within the boundaries of your possibilities. The thing you've never done could take you far afield of where you are or have been. Or it could mean that you stop doing something you've always done. It might be time to stop leading the parade and to teach someone else what you know.

Now is the time to examine the state of your wonder. Not only what do you wonder about; but do you wonder at all? Curiosity is the most valuable tool you have for maintaining a lively mind. When you run out of questions is when you'll be old.

Part of your personal assessment will reveal that the physical and financial changes that were emerging during your 60s are now very clear. Have you embraced them, made room for them? For within these boundaries you will find the scope to which Hamilton refers. It is within that scope that you can dare to try whatever your "something you've never done" will be.

Last of all, examine how open your life is. There are seasons of birth in our lives and seasons of loss. The losses come more often with time, and you must continually sow the seeds of new friendships of all ages; for relationships are the nourishment of our lives.

And, now that you are 70, plan on being 80, like me.

On Composing a Life
by Elaine Madsen

Inside every old person there's a young one
wondering, "What the hell happened?" I don't.
Because I know. Exactly what happened.
I lived, I wept, I failed, and reinvented myself
more times than I knew I could; lived in a
mansion and in two little rooms and in
everything in between.

When I was very young, I couldn't find people
who had anything to say so I manufactured some
— three of them.
Because of these three children, I've had
more life to live on some singular days
than some live in a lifetime.

I've known great love and loss
and grief much more intimately
than I'd ever have wished,
but in its darkness I discovered
the riveting end to the argument
I once had with God.

I've been composing the symphony
of my life for 80 years.
I'm now on the theatre movement
with no last movement in sight.

6

Being Present: A Way to Live More Fully

by Boyd Lemon

After a stellar 40-year career as a nationally recognized attorney, Boyd Lemon discovered his passion — writing — and pursued it in many venues: in the idyllic coastal town of Ventura, California; in the literary, art, and music scenes of Boston; on the Left Bank in Paris, where he lived for one bohemian year; and, finally, by the bucolic rivers and forests of St. Marys, Georgia, where he currently lives. Lemon's newest book is *Retirement: A Memoir and Guide*. He has published six other books and is now working on his first novel. His second passion is travel, and he has visited six of the seven continents. He has four adult children and four grandchildren.

One of the advantages and joys of retirement is having the time to figure out some things that you just couldn't focus on when you were working full-time — such as how to live more fully. One way is to "be present" or "live in the moment" as much as possible. When you are present, you notice and find joy in the beauty around you that you never noticed before. It really works, but you have to make the effort because most of us have spent years living outside the present moment — planning or worrying about the future, regretting or reminiscing about the past. The first time I was aware of another person "being present" was while talking with a woman whom I had just met. There was conversation all around her, and her attention was not on me. But when I asked her a question, she turned to look at me and proceeded to give an in-depth answer, which took several minutes. During that time, she continued looking straight at me, concentrating totally on what she was saying as well as my reaction. Weeks later, while I was eating dinner with a friend, I noticed that the reason she didn't converse much was because she was savoring every bite of her meal. When either of us talked, she stopped eating in order to be intently engaged in the conversation. Without trying, these two women taught me what being present is.

The more we practice being present, the less frequently our minds will wander back to the past or forward to the future. I practice observing everything around me wherever I am — just *being*. I practice when I am doing mundane, everyday tasks. When I brush my teeth, rather than daydream or think about what I am going to do that day, I become fully focused on brushing my teeth, noticing exactly where I am brushing, what it feels like, what it tastes and smells like, and the sound that it makes. When I do the dishes, I try to concentrate totally on that, rather than letting my mind drift off to some other thought. When I walk on the beach, unless the purpose of my walk is to think about something, I try not to think of anything except what I see, hear, and smell on the beach. What a difference from when I used to walk on the beach without paying attention — afterwards I could barely even remember the walk! Being present is experiencing life; anything else is less.

Living in the moment 100 percent of the time, even if possible, would invite disaster for all but cloistered monks. Sometimes, it's necessary to plan future activities or to think about what we've learned in the past in order to solve current problems or to avoid immediate threats to our well-being. But clinging sentimentally to the unending stream of items that have flowed through our lives detracts from the joy of living in the here and now. We must find a balance that works for each one of us, taking the past and future into account without letting them override our enjoyment of the present.

7

Some Men Drink. Some Men Womanize. I Play the Trombone.

by Samuel Jay Keyser

Samuel Jay Keyser, special assistant to the chancellor at MIT, is professor emeritus in the Department of Linguistics and Philosophy. Aside from his career in theoretical linguistics, he plays trombone with the avant-garde Aardvark Jazz Orchestra and on a fire truck with a Dixieland ensemble, the New Liberty Jazz Band. A book about traveling with his wife, Nancy Kelly, entitled I *Married a Travel Junkie*, appeared in 2012, as did a memoir, *Mens et Mania: The* MIT *Nobody Knows*. His children's book, *The Pond God and Other Stories*, received a Lee Bennett Hopkins Honor Award for children's poetry in 2004.

William Congreve's play *The Mourning Bride* opens famously with the line, "Music has charms to soothe a savage breast." Had I lived in 1697, the year the play premiered, I would have said those words were written for me. When my first marriage was falling to pieces, I didn't womanize. I didn't take to drink. I took up the trombone.

I had played the horn when I was much younger. But as Corinthians 13:11 says, "When I was a child . . . I thought as a child: but when I became a man, I put away childish things." I put away my horn. It stayed in its case for 30 years. Then my marriage went south. Why did I reach for that horn again? I don't know. Call it instinct — the way elephants in Africa chew on the walls of caves when they need salt.

At first, playing comforted me, like a baby sucking its thumb. Gradually, it became its own reward. Now, at the age of 77, 20 years after the divorce, I find myself in the New Liberty Jazz Band playing Dixieland tunes like "Kid Ory's Creole Trombone" from the bed of a 1941 Ford fire truck — all because of a marriage gone bust.

Before I joined the band, two of the players had spotted the truck rusting in a field. Its owner, a farmer, was going to turn it into a hay wagon. A $400 offer convinced him otherwise. My fellow musicians were also, among other things, highly skilled auto mechanics. They outfitted the truck with speakers, a mixing board, microphones, a canopy, and chairs welded to the frame for safety. It rose up out of the ashes a shiny red mobile bandstand. I relate to that fire truck. Its rebirth foreshadowed my second marriage, to Nancy Kelly. Who would have guessed that my endgame would be my best game?

There is nothing like sitting atop the fire truck on First Night in Boston, rolling up Boylston Street playing "Struttin' with Some Barbecue" while a million people cheer at the top of their lungs. It isn't that we are that good. It's just that on First Night, which is both the last night of the old year and the first night of the new, you could play a B-flat scale and everyone would think you were wonderful.

Congreve knew what he was talking about.

I play in another band, the Aardvark Jazz Orchestra. It is an avant-garde jazz orchestra. The New York City Jazz Record designated Aardvark's latest CD, Evocations, as one of the five best large-jazz-ensemble releases of 2012. The average age of our band members is somewhere around 50. If you were to take me out of the mix, it would plummet. Is my presence making the band older or me younger? That is a no-brainer.

Here's the bottom line: a problem is not just a problem.

It is the first step in a solution, a solution that can take you to a place you never imagined you would ever go. Think of it as buying an airplane ticket and not knowing the destination. It doesn't matter. It's the getting there that counts.

8

Turning 70!

by Dorian Mintzer, M.S.W., Ph.D.

Dorian Mintzer, M.S.W., Ph.D., board-certified coach, is a licensed psychologist, career/life transition coach, couples relationship coach, executive coach, consultant, writer, speaker, and teacher. She facilitates workshops and speaks to community, corporate, and professional groups on topics related to midlife and second-half-of-life issues. Mintzer is founder of the Boomers and Beyond Special Interest Group for Interdisciplinary Professionals and the fourth Tuesday at noon (EST) Retirement Interview Series for professionals and the public. She is coauthor with Roberta Taylor of *The Couple's Retirement Puzzle: The 10 Must-Have Conversations for Transitioning to the Second Half of Life* and a contributing author to *Six Secrets to a Happy Retirement, Live Smart After 50!, 65 Things to Do When You Retire,* and *65 Things to Do When You Retire: Travel.* You can learn more about Mintzer (and sign up for her interview series) at revolutionizeretirement.com. Learn more about *The Couple's Retirement Puzzle* at couplesretirementpuzzle.com.

The prospect of turning 70 may bring excitement and also possibly fear. From my perspective, 70 is not the new 50; it's the new 70. Some people are still working and, if not full-time, doing something — whether paid or unpaid — that hopefully gives purpose and meaning to their lives and provides an opportunity for engagement and connection.

Many people in their 70s are in relationships — with the same person they've been with for many years or perhaps with a new person, in a new marriage or living arrangement. And others are single — divorced, widowed, or never married. The divorce rate for the over-50 population has been increasing. There are older individuals who decide they don't want to be married, often preferring to be "in relationship" but not to live together. There's also a phenomenon called "Living Apart Together (LAT)" where couples are fully committed to each other but recognize their differing needs and spend some part of the year living separately. At a recent workshop, a participant mentioned that in too many marriages people are "living together but apart," that is, still living together but emotionally disconnected. It's vital to be in touch with what is meaningful to you.

If you're in a relationship — married or unmarried, it's also necessary to learn what's important to your partner — so you can fulfill aspects of your individual vision as well as create a "shared vision" with your significant other. Communication is crucial. By now, you've hopefully found ways to communicate with your partner and also with other key people in your life, whether they're siblings, other relatives, adult children, grandchildren, or great-grandchildren. But sometimes the most crucial conversations we need to have with our partners at this time of life may also be the hardest ones for us to have. It's helpful to open up space for the "we" of the relationship so you can discuss important issues, and compromise and problem-solve together.

Although we can't control everything in life, there is certainly a lot we *can* control. Appreciate your own life, and the perspective and wisdom that you have gained from confronting life's challenges. If you reach 70 and haven't yet had "end of life" discussions with your partner or people who are important to you, *don't put it off.* It may feel scary, but it can also be freeing and empowering to make your wishes and needs clear, both verbally and in writing. There are a variety of legal forms to understand and fill out, such as a health-care proxy, a durable power of attorney, and HIPAA forms, as well as a current will, estate planning, etc. In addition, you have the chance to say what you do — and don't — want at the end of your life and how, if possible, you'd like to end your life when it's time. Some people think this is morbid and is a subject to be avoided. I think it's actually "an act of love" to confront these issues and to let those you love know what's most important to you. As we so often hear, life is not a dress rehearsal. We have an incredible opportunity to live life fully to the end and to be conscious and intentional in how we live these wonderful years.

9

Old Girl — New Dress

by Barbara Boldt

Barbara Boldt was born in Germany in 1930 and came of age in wartime Europe. After World War II, she immigrated to Canada, married, and raised a family before learning to paint in her mid-40s. She embraced this late career as the work and passion of her life, and through her paintings explores the world around her, the vanishing landscapes of British Columbia's Fraser Valley, and the intricate rock forms of the Gulf Islands. *Places of Her Heart: The Art and Life of Barbara Boldt*, by K. Jane Watt in conversation with Boldt, was published by Fenton Street Press in 2012.

I am a painter who is now almost 83. Two months after my 70th birthday, my daughter, Dorothy, died. For me, that year was an important step in the journey I'm taking. Realization came to me to make use of the time I've got left. I knew that I needed to do my own work, but I also needed to find a way to serve the talented artist that my daughter was. I am working on a series of 45 paintings in honor of her life.

After Dorothy died, I moved away from my small, downtown living space to a place in the country, hoping to find new energy, new inspiration. I am teaching here, still welcoming a swarm of women into my house each Wednesday. This coterie of painters keeps me going. They bring the world in to me — and they help me make a living!

I continue to see beauty in the world around me, and I want to record it in one way or another — sometimes in pictures, but most often in words. I still love to work in my studio, a place where I can shut out the cares of the world and just paint, paint, paint. Many years ago, I wrote about my studio. Time has not changed the feeling of peace I get from working there, listening to classical music:

My studio means so much to me . . . I have made it my own with my soul in it — when I go to work in the morning, it is with joy and expectation. I am coming into my space. My easel and the tools of my trade, my paintings surrounding me — everything is there because I want it there.

As we age, we need to withdraw from some activities, but not from living, not from seeing what is so good about life. Last year, I was able — through the generosity of a good friend — to publish my memoir and to catalogue the paintings I have done over the last 30 years. K. Jane Watt, the writer who was working with me, asked me why I paint. Why do I paint? I answered: "There is so much art in me. If you have a voice, you want to sing it. You want to do what you can do. I'm that same way. It makes me feel good. It makes me feel like me."

10

Gather Together!

by Ellen Cole, Ph.D., and Jane Giddan, M.A., CCC-SLP

Ellen Cole, Ph.D., professor emerita of psychology at Alaska Pacific University in Anchorage, is currently teaching at the College of St. Rose in Albany, New York, the Albany Academies, and Union Institute and University. Her latest book, edited with Mary Gergen, is *Retiring but Not Shy: Feminist Psychologists Create Their Post-Careers* (Taos Institute, 2012).

Jane Giddan, M.A., CCC-SLP, professor emerita of the Department of Psychiatry, University of Toledo Health Sciences Center, is a speech-language pathologist who has specialized in language development and disorders. She is the coauthor of numerous articles and books regarding autism and communication in child mental health.

Pals since childhood, Cole and Giddan created the blog 70candles.com, and have conducted "conversation groups" throughout the U.S. for women in their 70s. They are writing a book, *70Candles Women!*, about this rich era in women's lives.

U s, 70? Could it be? Here we were, two lifelong friends, reunited geographically on the U.S. mainland. We could now visit more easily and share the next era of our lives, but what did we know about being "old"? We wished for a road map for the years ahead, but knew of none. What were other women in their eighth decade doing? What were their hopes and dreams? We decided to find out.

We began by reviewing the relevant literature, and found that it focused largely on ill health and depression; hardly any of it described the vitality of the older women we knew and hoped to be. We decided to reach beyond ourselves by starting a blog, 70candles.com. It began:

Women everywhere, welcome to our blogspot, a space for sharing experiences, thoughts, and ideas about how to thrive as we approach and endure in the eighth decade of life. We hope this exchange will be a source of inspiration for the next generation of 70-year-olds. . . . What has this transition been like for you? Serious, funny, commonplace, unusual, short, long stories all welcome. How does it feel to be among the oldest in the crowd? What does it take to thrive in this decade? How do you think others see you? What contributes to well-being and, yes, flourishing, at three score and ten?

The posts arrived slowly at first, but soon women began to talk and lend support to each other on our site. Those reaching their 70th birthday, idly searching the Web for comfort, found us and shared feelings about that emotional moment. Women posted serious and funny anecdotes; tales about ageism, retirement struggles, and financial calamities and solutions; and some wonderful poetry. Many offered encouragement, and spoke of new explorations, gratitude, and resilience. The entries were rich with honest emotions, sensitivity, and good humor.

We began to wonder, what if we organized conversation groups for women in their 70s, to discuss this new, uncharted decade face-to-face? Would our age-mates, many of them proud participants in the feminist encounter groups of the '60s, be willing to gather together again? We gave it a go, and to date have held 70Candles gatherings in New York, Pennsylvania, and Texas. What moving and humor-filled discussions have ensued! Women our age seem to love talking about this time of life. We share common joys and challenges, and we welcome the chance to speak about topics rarely aired.

Our blog and conversation groups have had an unexpected positive effect on our own lives. They have provided us with the key elements described by George Vaillant, Dan Gilbert, and virtually every researcher who examines human happiness and positive aging: we're embedded in a cause larger than ourselves, we're expanding our social networks and bonds with others, and we're thrust into new learning as we manage technological challenges on the Web. We've gained a new respect for being 70. We are proud, vital, engaged, and unabashedly old women!

Reference:
Vaillant, G. (2004). Positive aging. In P. A. Linley & S. Joseph (Eds.), *Positive psychology in practice* (pp. 561–578). New York: Wiley.

||

Write Your Life

by Judy F. Kugel

Judy F. Kugel is associate dean of students at Harvard's John F. Kennedy School of Government, where she has worked in a variety of capacities for 33 years. She holds a B.A. in Government from the University of Michigan and an M.Ed. from Boston College. Kugel has an ongoing interest in career choices and life's transitions and has taught workshops on both subjects. She has published numerous personal essays and travel articles, but now spends most of her writing efforts on *The 70-Something Blog* at 70-something.com, which she started in order to document her own transition into her 70s.

You're 70. Do you want to enrich your eighth decade? Write. Write fiction or nonfiction, poetry or prose. Write a memoir or a blog. But write. If not now, when?

In your 70s, writing can take on a new purpose. Use it to help you process your life. Or to leave a legacy for those who love you.

I've been writing my life for years. I write about things I want to remember and things I'd rather forget. I still have a hastily scribbled journal of giving birth to my first child 43 years ago. I write when someone I love goes through a trauma, to help me cope with the anxiety.

I often record transitions in my life. I wrote a daily journal when I was 59 because I thought turning 60 would be monumental. (It wasn't.) I wrote a short "autobiography" of my youth when our children asked us to write about what things were like in the "olden days." And I write a "letter" to my young grandchildren, Leo and Grady, after our visits (every two months) that I hope will help them remember their grandparents years from now.

Five years ago, when I was about to turn 70, I decided to document the coming decade. Instead of writing just for myself, I started a blog. I wanted to share the ups and downs of aging. I thought I would write about my own parents and being a parent, about the role that exercise plays in my life, about my job and being an "older" worker. And, of course, I planned to write about my aging body.

For the past five years, I have blogged twice a week.

Every single week. My blog posts rarely exceed 300 words. Utter strangers read them. And they comment. Some tell me that what I write resonates with them. Others tell me my experiences help them prepare to be 70. And some of my younger readers tell me that they like knowing that life can be very good as one ages. Most important, the writing is immensely satisfying to me.

So, go ahead and join the 200 million people blogging. Blog about what interests you. Jane Austen? Old movies? The environment? Politics? Your life?

Here's how. First you need to register the name of your blog. You can do that for as little as $5 to a domain provider. Then, you need a host — an organization that will give you space on its server. You can pay a host for a space (I use Typepad) or get it free (Blogger and WordPress.com are two popular host sites). The more you pay, the more services you get.

Tell your relatives and friends about your blog. If they like it, they'll tell their friends. If you are on Facebook, announce it and post a link to your blog. Commit to write regularly to keep your readers coming back to see what you have to say.

In my first five years, I wrote 520 posts. When I started, my family members were my only readers. Now, I have readers all over the world.

Go ahead. Write your life!

12

Learn from the Oldest and Most Vibrant People in America

by Gwen Weiss-Numeroff

Gwen Weiss-Numeroff is a nutritionist, professional speaker, and award-winning author. After witnessing too many loved ones die prematurely from various diseases, she went on a two-year quest to learn the secrets to vital longevity from some of America's oldest and most spirited people. In her book *Extraordinary Centenarians in America: Their Secrets to Living a Long Vibrant Life*, 30 remarkable people reveal what it took for them to live a long, healthy, and happy life, sharing everything from their diets to physical activities, current interests, and other lifestyle choices, so that readers can incorporate these healthy habits into their own lives.

Although I am only 49, I am blessed to have learned so much about life at 70 years (and beyond) from an amazing group of older Americans. While interviewing these folks for my book

Extraordinary Centenarians in America: Their Secrets to Living a Long Vibrant Life, I was extremely curious about how they had remained busy, fulfilled, and healthy. After all, they must have been doing something right, since they lived for an additional three joyful decades.

1. Have a purpose.

Never run out of responsibility; if you don't have one, find one. Find a cause and knock yourself out for it. It will enhance your brainpower and interest in life, and keep you alive longer.
— Alyse Laemmle, life insurance agent, 96

This wise, generous, and witty lady had her best year in insurance sales at 96. Like the majority of nonagenarians and centenarians I had the pleasure of meeting, Alyse stated that, in one's 70s and beyond, it is very important to have a purpose. This could mean a form of work, whether it's the same profession as in earlier years, something completely different, or perhaps both. By their 70s, these interviewees were fortunate enough to no longer need to work for monetary compensation, but they experienced numerous other benefits: maintaining a keen, alert mind; fostering connections with new, possibly interesting people; and the enjoyment and intrigue of a fresh challenge.

Volunteering is another meaningful option. Serving about two hours per week is particularly beneficial to the health of older adults, due to the sense of accomplishment from these activities. Recent studies have shown that volunteers have greater longevity, higher functional ability, lower rates of depression, and lower incidence of heart disease. Basically, it does you good to be good to others! It can significantly improve the quantity and quality of your years.

2. Explore new places, have escapades, take up hobbies.

My mother rode a camel and a mechanical bull, flew in a hot-air balloon, and traveled the world two dozen times in her later years.

— daughter of 104-year-old Anne LoMedico

Most of the centenarians embraced their well-earned freedom by exploring new hobbies and places, and going on adventures around the world. If you're a bit tamer than Anne LoMedico, here are some less audacious activities: join or start a book club, study a new language, or learn to play a new instrument. Then, visit a country where the language you learned is spoken or where one of your book-club selections was set. Take up knitting, write poetry or mysteries, start gardening, or learn how to make sushi or some other ethnic cuisine. The world is open for you to explore, and there are classes available for almost anything.

3. Go with the tide and be grateful.

This was the most important lesson I learned from my centenarian friends. Although they faced mountains of difficulties throughout a century of experiences, the most common mantra among them was to "go with the tide." They did not bemoan life's obstacles and were grateful for what they had, no matter how little. This mindset enabled them to triumph over their challenges with strength, grace, dignity, and joy.

13

"Dorothy, We're Not in Kansas Anymore . . . " — "The Times They Are A-Changin'"

by Maribeth Colloton

Maribeth Colloton is the writer/creator/CEB ("Chief Executive Boomer") of BoomerGrandparents.com. A Midwest transplant to Northern California, Colloton founded the award-winning blog BoomerGrandparents.com after the birth of her first granddaughter. Faced with boredom after a job layoff, the challenge of creating a blog became a welcome remedy. Embracing today's technology, and motivated by a strong desire to maintain relationships, Colloton was determined to learn about her networking options. Social media sites such as Facebook, Twitter, LinkedIn, and FaceTime are providing a positive tool for remaining connected with out-of-state family members, old and new friends, and her delightful grandchildren.

C lose your eyes. Think back to your first day of high school, and try to remember your emotions. *Fear:* How do I find my locker, and will I be able to open it? Will I be able to find any of my friends? *Excitement:* There are interesting classes to take, new people to meet, and clubs and sports to participate in. *Awe:* It's so big! Nothing is familiar! There are so many people! There is so much to *learn*.

The feelings you had on that first day of high school are probably not much different from how you felt the first time someone asked you to e-mail them, call them on a cell phone, send them a text message, or "like" them on Facebook. Technology often evokes *fear, excitement,* and *awe* in those of us who grew up with rotary phones, a set of encyclopedias, written letters, and face-to-face communication with friends and family. But remember: had you never opened those high school doors, there would have been no new friends, your knowledge would have been limited, and your future would have been less full of wonder, accomplishment, and pride — similar to the repercussions for choosing NOT to embrace the technology available to you today.

As the title of Bob Dylan's song from 1964 says, "The

Times They Are A-Changin'." Did he really comprehend how true his words would be? The extent of change that technology has presented to our generation is incomprehensible. Accepting and exploring social media as septuagenarians enables us to challenge our minds and improve our lives on so many levels. After all, in 70+ years we've met many people, and we have life experiences that need sharing.

Communication vehicles such as e-mail, texting, Facebook, and Skype are like highways to our kids and grandkids. No matter where they are on the planet, today's grandparents have the ability to maintain close relationships with their grandchildren from birth through adulthood. The saying "Grandchildren are a grandparent's link to the future, and grandparents are a child's link to the past" becomes so much more real with the connective power of social media. The look of awe on my grandchildren's faces when I told them there were no computers or cell phones when I was little was priceless. Hearing my grandson call me "Mimi" for the first time while using Skype's face-to-face technology would have sounded like something out of *The Twilight Zone*, and was a magic moment I would have missed, had I not chosen to take a class or watch an online tutorial. In turn, I look forward to my grandchildren opening doors to even newer technological advances that will enhance our ability to connect.

Whether you are a beginner or an experienced user of new technology, instructional resources are available, via online tutorials or classes offered by community and senior centers, neighborhood schools, and colleges. The benefits of embracing technology will far surpass any hesitation you may feel about taking that initial step.

So, overcome your fears, just like you did that first day of high school, when you got your locker opened.

14

Sometimes 70 Is Just 70

by Marshall P. Duke, Ph.D.

Marshall P. Duke, Charles Howard Candler Professor of Psychology at Emory University, graduated from Rutgers University in 1964 and completed his Ph.D. in clinical psychology at Indiana University in 1968. After two years of service in the U.S. Army Medical Service Corps, he joined the Emory faculty in 1970. An award-winning teacher, he has also published over 100 research articles and nine books. A regular contributor to the Huffington Post, he has appeared on *Good Morning America*, TODAY, and *The Oprah Winfrey Show*. Professor Duke and his wife, Sara Bookman Duke, have three children and nine grandchildren.

Most readers of fiction will tell you that they often come upon a line in a book or a song that hits them squarely and brings them pause. I can remember how meaningful the Beatles' song "When I'm 64" was to me when I was 64, how I sang it on my birthday, how its lyrics resonated with me. But now, at 70 — the "terribly strange" age in Paul

Simon's song "Old Friends" — I turn to a line uttered by Max Roby, a 70-year-old character in Richard Russo's Pulitzer Prize–winning novel, *Empire Falls*.

In the made-for-TV version of this book, Max Roby was played by Paul Newman, who captured the feistiness of the character perfectly. In a particularly engaging scene, Max is having a meal with his son, Miles. In the course of the conversation, Miles says to Max, "You've got Cheetos in your beard." Max then delivers the line that engaged me so. He replies simply, "So what?"

In the book, once he gets past the shock of his father's answer, Miles thinks to himself:

> Max had a point . . . and was probably right. People were just themselves, their efforts to be otherwise notwithstanding. Max was just programmed to be Max, to have food in his beard. Looked at from another angle, it probably was admirable that his father never battled his own nature, never expected more of himself than experience had taught him was wise, thereby avoiding disappointment and self-recrimination. It was a fine, sensible way to live.

Had I read Miles's thoughts about not battling one's own nature when I was a student in a Skinnerian behaviorist laboratory in the 1960s, I would have railed against it. But I have now battled my own nature for 70 years, and I believe I have learned that I was naïve.

I am not blind to the importance of nurture; it is a powerful force. My concern is with the growing belief that nature can be overridden, that it can be set aside, overcome. We seem to believe, for example, that naturally aggressive children can be transformed into angelic playmates, that naturally shy children can become social butterflies, and that children with limited intellectual abilities can become intellectual powerhouses. Old people need not lose their cognitive capacities; 80-year-olds can climb Everest; 85-year-olds can finish a triathlon. Seventy, we are told, is the new 50.

I know that a number of older people don't lose their capacities; these people make the news. But a significant number do weaken and fade, despite every effort not to. Yet, as a culture, we often find ourselves blaming those whom nature has not favored for not rising above their biologically based limitations. The reality is this: if indeed there is a battle between nature and nurture, nurture may have its day, but in the long run, nature always wins. More often than not, 70 is simply 70. And this needs to be simply okay.

15

What Will I Be Doing When I Turn 70? Probably Not What I Am Doing Today

by Bob Lowry

Bob Lowry was a management consultant to several hundred radio stations before retiring in 2001. He has written two books, including *Living a Satisfying Retirement*, his latest, and he's contributed to *65 Things to Do When You Retire* and *65 Things to Do When You Retire: Travel* (both published by Sellers Publishing). Lowry authors a successful retirement blog and lives with his wife in Scottsdale, Arizona. Visit his Web site at satisfyingretirement.com.

Being 6 years short of the 70-year mark, I am left to speculate. But, if the past dozen years of my retirement life are any clue, I am pretty sure I know what I won't be doing when I turn 70: much of what I am doing now. For experience has taught me that we can't predict what new paths may open up to us — if we allow ourselves to be open to them.

After a rather prosaic and predictable life filled with the usual stops for college, marriage, children, and career, the last thing I expected upon retirement was any major change in my life. My interests, attitudes and opinions, political views, even my hobbies and how I spent my leisure time, were "normal." My lifestyle was safe and steady. Surprises were few.

Starting a few years after retirement, things began to change. My routine became too routine. I chafed at what had become a pattern of unfulfilling activities. Too much reading and too many nights spent in front of the television left me feeling empty. For the first time, I began to sense the passage of time. My days, then weeks, and finally whole months would slip away without my being able to recall accomplishing anything in particular.

I have no idea what the trigger was, but about three years into retirement I realized I was wasting the most precious of all gifts we are given: time. In a burst of energy — and with a fresh perspective — I began to experiment with new hobbies and interests. My wife and I agreed to downsize our living quarters, to simplify our lives, and to try new things. We both trained to become spiritual counselors and spent six years helping those who were struggling with emotional, physical, or medical problems.

As someone who had not been very empathetic before, these years opened my eyes. I realized I had both the skills and the desire to help others. This led me to prison ministry, which has been a central focus of my life for the past five years. It was terrifying at first, and I found myself stepping completely out of my comfort zone. However, working with men in prison has become a defining change in my life.

I also feel a new sense of achievement. For the past three years, I have taken my lifelong love of writing from a dream to reality. A successful blog about retirement has led to a travel book and two published works on retirement. I have found the creative outlet that I have needed but avoided for far too many years.

I am not the same person I once was. Yes, my core values and spiritual beliefs remain pretty much unchanged. But, with each passing year, I seem to find something new to explore or try on for size. My interests at 64 weren't even on my radar at 54. I am confident that when I turn 70 I will be moving in several new directions that I can't even envision today. That uncertainty is what keeps me so excited about the future. There really are no limits.

16

Be a Detective!

by Patricia Rockwell, Ph.D.

Patricia Rockwell, Ph.D., is the author of two mystery series and the founder of Cozy Cat Press. Her Essie Cobb Senior Sleuth mysteries include *Bingoed*, *Papoosed*, *Valentined*, and *Ghosted*. Rockwell based her heroine — feisty 90-year-old detective Essie Cobb — on her own mother, a curious and adventurous lady who lived to 91. Dr. Rockwell spent most of her career teaching. Her Ph.D. is from the University of Arizona. She was on the faculty at the University of Louisiana at Lafayette for 13 years and retired in 2007. Dr. Rockwell is presently living in Aurora, Illinois, with her husband, Milt, also a retired educator.

I haven't quite reached 70, and my fictional character, Essie Cobb, passed that marker years ago, so we view this magical age from two different directions. Nevertheless, both Essie and I would offer the exact same advice to someone turning 70: "Be a detective!"

Essie says it because she's been detecting mysteries at the Happy Haven Assisted Living Facility for many years. Essie knows that "being a detective" involves curiosity and love of adventure — qualities that Essie possesses aplenty. In the four books in which she has appeared (*Bingoed, Papoosed, Valentined,* and *Ghosted*), Essie makes each day count as she focuses all her energy on tracking down clues and solving problems — activities that also help keep her engaged and happy at her advanced age.

From my perspective as the author of Essie's books, I also see life as a test of my detecting skills. When I retired from a satisfying career as a college professor a few years ago, I thought I would spend my retirement relaxing. It took me about two days to discover that I was thoroughly bored. So, having been a lifelong mystery reader, I put on my detecting hat to determine what I could do with my new life. It turned out the answer was right in front of me. All those murder mysteries I'd been reading began to call to me. Maybe I could write one myself.

I began to write my first book. When it was completed, I tried submitting the book to a traditional publisher, but it went the way of most new authors' manuscripts — onto the junk pile. My detecting instinct told me that it might be possible to produce the book myself, because the new independent publishing movement was just starting to gather steam. More detecting was required: what was involved in self-publishing a book? This, it turned out, was almost as big a job as writing a mystery. But I forged ahead, just like any good sleuth. Of course, there were a few false starts — as most detectives probably experience — but ultimately, Cozy Cat Press was born.

In the end, I had detected a way to make my retirement satisfying. Soon, other "cozy" mystery authors began submitting manuscripts to me. I became an editor — a job that was much like being a teacher. Today, as I look back on the last few years, it's hard to believe that I'm the editor and publisher of a small but thriving publishing company.

So, when I say that Essie Cobb, fictional sleuth, and Patricia Rockwell, real-life publisher, are both detectives, I mean it in the broadest sense. Whether you're closing in on 70 (as I am) or seeing it from your rearview mirror (as Essie does), you know that being a detective means you always have to be curious about all that life has to offer.

17

The Septuagenarian Challenge

by Rick Kimball

Richard S. (Rick) Kimball is a Maine-based freelance writer and photographer. He and his wife, Tirrell, own and operate Green Timber Publications, a small press producing religious education curricula for use in Unitarian Universalist congregations. Kimball began his writing and editing career as a reporter, columnist, and city editor at what was then the Guy Gannett newspapers of Portland, Maine. He next became a full-time writer and editor for J. Weston Walch, Publisher, producing supplementary educational materials for secondary schools. He has written religious education material for the national Unitarian Universalist Association and in the areas of creativity, local history, and human sexuality. He holds a B.A. from Harvard College and an M.A. from Columbia University Graduate School of Journalism.

Sixty-nine is a great age. Look at the number: 69. It reads the same right-side-up and upside-down. We can see it just as well whether standing on our feet or on our hands. We won't get another number that good until we reach 88.

Seventy has less graphic appeal but offers richer rewards. Accepting the common if not crisply accurate wisdom that the body replaces itself every seven years, then on our 70th birthday we complete our 10th life and begin the 11th. That's two more than a cat gets and the starting point for the septuagenarian challenge: knowing how best to enjoy and to repay the universe for this dividend of time.

The answer grows out of the knowledge that aging is a subtractive art. Think Shakespeare: sans teeth, sans eyes, sans taste, heading toward sans everything. If I were to meet the Bard I might suggest adding sans memory, but that's not the point. The key truth is this, that our eighth decade allows us to become our genuine selves. Like a good simmering broth, we reduce to essence. Before finally boiling away, sans everything, we become our own key ingredient of fulfillment.

We spend the first decades of our lives individuating, finding ourselves as separate egos. We can continue that process in our 70s, but should first focus on the vital human essence that unites and defines us as a species: creative power.

Creativity gives and makes us gods. Creativity lets us shape and build our world. Creativity separates us from the fauna that may create dams and hives and nests, but always without thought, without "neo design," without decoration. Creativity gives us connective reason for continuing life.

Meeting the septuagenarian challenge requires just this: creation. So take the challenge, and make something new, something different. If you are already a writer, sculpt. If you are already a musician, dig a garden plot. If you are already a cook, go to an art museum and buy a set of paints in the gift shop. Channel Grandma Moses.

But first things first. Here's the critical first step into the septuagenarian decade: create nonsense.

On your 70th birthday — or the day after that if you're too exhausted from blowing out candles — write at least an hour's worth of nonsense. Do it by longhand or computer, use fresh words or old, make it rhyme or not, but do it. Nonsense lies beyond judgment.

It smothers the sounds of I *can't*, I *don't know how*, I'm *not creative*. With those voices silenced, you are ready to create something more, to live out life's purpose, to make your own destiny. Dare you ask for anything else? No, but you can get it anyway.

Here's the bonus: having written nonsense, real, honest makes-no-sense-but-still-feels-good nonsense, you are ready to run for Congress or any other elective body that might appeal for your 70s. But that step is not necessary to meeting the septuagenarian challenge. The sole essential is creation, the spark of all life.

18

I CAME, I LAUGHED, I LEARNED

by Madeleine Kolb

Madeleine Kolb is a Seattle-based freelance writer, blogger, and speaker with extensive experience in the public and private sectors. She has degrees in zoology and genetics and a certificate in technical writing, all from the University of Washington. On her blog at agemyths.com, Kolb writes about the myths and realities of aging and related topics. Her writer's portfolio is at cheshirecatcommunications.com. Some years ago, she ventured into her first Toastmasters meeting and found it far more supportive than she'd imagined. Now a Distinguished Toastmaster (DTM), she highly recommends the organization to people of all ages.

It was a day to remember: December 17, 2003, the 100th anniversary of the first powered flight. There I was, telling the story in a large meeting room filled with engineers. Projected on a screen behind me were photographs of Orville and Wilbur Wright flying over the sands at Kitty Hawk.

The audience was rapt, and I was exhilarated. I couldn't have done it without Toastmasters!

Like many other people, I used to become anxious at the mere thought of public speaking, so when I heard about Toastmasters I promised myself that I'd check it out. Some day.

And I did. I went online and found a club that met on Wednesday evenings in the basement of a church near where I live in Seattle. On the appointed day, I set out. At the time, I didn't know what to expect, but it most certainly wasn't what I encountered: a well-organized meeting with friendly people laughing and enjoying themselves while learning to become good speakers. I was impressed!

The next week, I went back. Before long, I built up enough courage to deliver my first speech. It became easier after that, and I went on to give speech after speech on topics as diverse as "Mad Cow Disease," "Dogs with Jobs," and "How to Do the Heimlich Maneuver" (I even used a human prop for this one).

The way to learn public speaking or any complex skill is to try it, get feedback (Toastmasters call it "evaluation"), try it again, get more feedback, and so on.

Whatever you call it, though, feedback can be nerve-wracking. As Woody Allen once said, "I love feedback. I just don't want to step in any."

But it's not like that in Toastmasters. An evaluator tells a speaker what she did well and offers supportive suggestions to help her make the speech even better. It was wonderful to see how well this simple technique worked, to watch a speaker's confidence soar, and to hear my fellow Toastmasters telling their stories from the heart. Gradually, I too became not only a better speaker but also a good evaluator. It meant a lot to get this note from a fellow Toastmaster:

> Madeleine . . . One of the reasons I joined the club was because of the evaluations I heard you give when I visited the club. I heard the advice you gave people, and saw how much they were learning from you each week . . .

Learning to love interacting with audiences at Toastmasters also had a positive impact on my job at the FAA (Federal Aviation Administration). I had become so comfortable giving speeches that I was happy to volunteer to give training presentations when the agency needed someone to do it. Because my comfort level had soared, I also offered to give a presentation, celebrating the 100th anniversary of the Wright brothers' extraordinary accomplishment, to an auditorium filled with aeronautical engineers.

Several years ago, I entered a humorous-speech contest and won each of the first three rounds. The fact that I made it to the fourth and final round was a big thrill. I never imagined that someday I'd be entertaining a huge audience with one of my speeches when I first walked into that room in the basement of a church in Seattle.

Joining Toastmasters is a wonderful way to meet friendly, interesting, and supportive people aged 18 to 70+. It's "like Gold's Gym for the mind," in the words of one of my longtime TM friends. You learn a lot and have a great time doing it. If you're in your 70s, I'd urge you to do what I did: I came to a meeting, I laughed, I learned. And I'm still laughing and learning after all these years.

19

Musing on the Joys of Cronehood

by Joan Paulson Gage

In her 50 years as a journalist, Joan Paulson Gage has written for many national magazines and newspapers, including the "Hers" column in the *New York Times*, a monthly feature for *Country Living*, and articles for *Vogue*, *Good Housekeeping*, and *Ladies' Home Journal*, among others. Married to author Nicholas Gage, she has three adult children and (at last!) a granddaughter, Amalía. Since 2008, she has written about "travel, art, photography, and life after 60" on her blog, arollingcrone.blogspot.com. Upon turning 60, in February of 2001, she returned to her first love — painting.

When you turn 70, you can't consider yourself middle-aged any more. Let's face it, you're wicked old. Which doesn't sound great, but in ancient times the entry into cronehood, the third period of a woman's life — after maiden and mother — was fêted with ceremonies and rituals, because the crones were revered as wise women who could impart their knowledge to the tribe.

I used to think the best time of life was when children are young and future triumphs are still possible. But now I think that, if you're a woman and lucky enough to remain in good health, your cronehood is the best era, free of the drama, responsibilities, worries, and the insecurities of youth.

When women turn 50, they're likely to give their husbands a big cast-of-thousands celebration and ignore their own birthday. But when they turn 60, many of my friends celebrated themselves with the party or trip they'd always wanted.

At 60, women often channel the creative energy they spent on home, children, and jobs into some long-hidden passion — designing jewelry, writing a book, gardening, volunteering. They allow themselves to try the things they'd always dreamed of, but never had time to do. A friend of mine went from wife, mother, and chef to law student, then lawyer, then judge, then a state chief justice. After a run-in with cancer, she retired. Now, she's enrolled at Tufts University's veterinary school so that, at age 70+, she can fulfill her childhood dream and become a veterinarian. (And she relaxes with horseback riding and tap dancing!)

I, too, went the "find-your-passion-at-60" route and turned from journalism (although I still do it) to rediscover art, which was my college major. So, 12 years ago, I started taking lessons at the Worcester Art Museum, exhibited in some local shows, and even sold some paintings.

As long as I can get around, I intend to travel to places I've never been, take lots of photographs and transform them into paintings. Just before turning 70, I spent a night on a beach in Nicaragua, watching sea turtles hatch and head to the sea, following our lanterns. For my birthday, I took a culinary tour in Mexico with chef Susana Trilling, and witnessed the arrival of millions of monarch butterflies at the El Rosario sanctuary, the final stop on their annual fall migration from the Canadian provinces and northeastern U.S. — an amazing experience!

Since then, these "bucket list" experiences have been crowding in — some by design and others by happy accident. But the biggest and best came in 2011, when my first grandchild, a golden-eyed girl named Amalía, entered the world.

Hanging out with her and chasing her around have literally made me feel a decade younger. And no exotic bucket-list experience can compare with seeing the wonder on her face when I show her something for the first time: patting a horse, throwing stones in a lake, putting the angel on the Christmas tree. I'm rediscovering the beauty in everyday things through her eyes.

To see everything as if for the first time — that's what she's teaching me, and that's what this crone would like to pass on to the next generation.

20

Finding My Song

by Tom Bissinger

Tom Bissinger is editing his memoir, *The Fun House*, for publication. His other books include *Da Capo: Selected Writings 1967–2004*, *Just What Is*, *Walterland*, and *Thoughts in the Moment*. Among his plays are *Descartes' Blues*, *The Big Kapresh*, and *Dreams, Mothers, and Death*, and he also composes songs. He and his wife live on a farm outside of Philadelphia, Pennsylvania.

"You sing because, if you don't, you die, at least a little," which is what I told myself when I turned 70 because, as I recall, I was searching for a song that I could call my song, although how I would know it was my song I wouldn't know until the song came to me, and, in the meantime, I was singing as I had done all my life, starting as soon as I woke up, although I do recall that in my dreams I had sung duets with Mick Jagger and Louis Armstrong, though not at the same time, but individually and with great exuberance, cherishing these dreams because

89

they were so lifelike and pleasurable, as if I had popped a can of soda and the fizzy hiss that escaped was my throat giving voice to a song not unknown to me, and certainly not surprising to Mick or Louis because, as Freud and others have said, you play all the characters in your dreams, so the boyish hipster and the cool bopster personas were part of my song line, if I may refer to another tradition, but the song line I was seeking, the song I was searching for, was a song that came from one's bones, a song that you couldn't really work at and craft; perhaps, after you had felt it in your bones you could, but until then you were waiting for inspiration to kick in, and in the morning, after rising from my bed, I found myself singing known songs that I had cherished all my life, Broadway show songs and Cole Porter tunes and traditional songs from family life, "Doodlee Doo" and "Balling the Jack," and why a particular song would appear to my consciousness I didn't think important to find out; the main thing was to sing, and so I've learned this, now that I am past 70 and finding my way vocally, that it's best if I try to sing softer, go easier on my vocal chords, and not strain for effect or attempt to mirror another singer, say Sinatra's "Strangers in the Night" or Tony Bennett's

"The Best Is Yet to Come," romantic songs of my youth, swinging yet tender, a kind of music we're so devoid of today, but I may feel that way because, as one gets older, you mainly remember the songs you heard at 30 years of age or younger, and so I wondered, among all the other songs I already knew, how would I ever hear my song, and then shortly after turning 70, I did, at the beach, and it came pretty quickly, in a variety of rhythms in the key of C, and it goes like this: "They say that love's a drop of water / A grain of sand upon the shore / And every time you think you've lost it / There's more and more and more and more."

21

Now We Are 70

by Robert Rector

Robert Rector has worked in print journalism for more than 45 years. He began his career at the *San Francisco Examiner*, then worked at the *Los Angeles Herald Examiner* and the *Los Angeles Daily News* before spending 33 years at the *Los Angeles Times*, where he shared in three Pulitzer Prizes. Rector is currently a columnist for a chain of newspapers in suburban Los Angeles, where he resides.

As a child, my bedtime literature of choice was anything by A.A. Milne. I enjoyed the tales of Winnie the Pooh and Christopher Robin, but *Now We Are Six* was my favorite.

I was impatient to reach that magical age, to leave babyhood behind and step out into the world on voyages of discovery and adventure. And being six was wonderful. It would be another five years before television made an appearance in our house, so we built elaborate dream worlds instead, traveling as far as our imaginations would carry us.

I mention all this because I am now 70. I am frankly astounded. It doesn't seem very long ago that I was six and playing cowboys with the boy down the street. I don't feel 70. Friends say I don't look 70. If they did, of course, they would no longer be my friends.

Come to think of it, however, I do have a lot more doctor appointments nowadays. I have gained a few inches around my waist, and sometimes I forget where I put my keys. So it must be true that I really am 70.

At this age, you try to live each day to its fullest and make some sense of your journey. On reflection, mine's been a wonderful trip.

I was born 18 days after Pearl Harbor. I often wonder how my parents felt about bringing a child into a world engaged in a massive war. Were they worried? Were they scared? They never spoke of it. But they were made of stern stuff. My mother was abandoned in an orphanage at age two. My dad never knew his real father. They were married just as the Depression hit.

My life wasn't nearly as tough. My world was living the lyrics of a Beach Boys song. We surfed and took our girlfriends to proms. We were true to our school. The worst thing that happened to me in high school was flunking geometry. Since it was midterm, I had to find a course to finish out the year. I chose journalism. The rest is history.

Going to college was a slap in the face. I learned about injustice. I experienced cynicism, much of it directed at the middle class from which I came. Two years after I had been surfing in Newport Beach, I was arrested in a civil-rights demonstration on Market Street in San Francisco. Defeating impediments to equality was an epic moment in this country's history. We took part because, simply, it was the right thing to do.

So now we stand poised on the banks of the River Jordan or the River Styx, depending on how things work out. The sun is still above the horizon, though not by much. But I'm not ready to say goodbye quite yet. Like a six-year-old, I'm still searching for worlds to explore and adventures to be had.

After all, as George Bernard Shaw said, "We don't stop playing because we grow old. We grow old because we stop playing."

22

Secrets for Your Successful 70s

by Susan Kersley

Susan Kersley was a doctor who wanted to be more creative and experience a different life. She studied personal development and had extensive counseling training (including earning a master's degree) while still working as a doctor. She was introduced to coaching by reading the books of Louise Hay and Thomas Leonard and then trained as a coach. Kersley wrote a series of articles in the *British Medical Journal* about coaching in relation to the lives of doctors, and she has published several books for doctors about improving their work/life balance. She's also published books about how to prepare for retirement. Now she paints, writes, coaches, and enjoys life. Her Web sites are at getreadyforretirement.co.uk, thedoctorscoach.co.uk, and lifeaftermedicine.co.uk.

Turning 70 means the start of a new decade with new opportunities to finally do what you really want to do, to pursue dreams that may have been swept aside years ago because of demands on your time from family and work.

Enjoying life at 70 depends on having a positive mindset about what it's still possible for you to achieve. Yet it's also a time for reflection about what you have accomplished already.

At every age, you may be aware of certain physical limitations. However, it is your mind as well as your body that can sometimes prevent you from doing all that you want to do. Don't allow yourself to feel trapped in a mindset of what you can't do. Believe in your own abilities!

If you are motivated and determined, you will find a way to succeed in spite of getting older. You now have increased wisdom, which will enable you to cope with situations that may have upset you before. This is the time to enjoy your family and friends, and to reconnect with those with whom you have lost touch.

It's so important as you reach your 70s to look after yourself and to do things you enjoy. Let go of activities that bore you and pursue those things that you love to do. Be creative: paint, draw, write. Keep active: walk, dance, practice yoga. Exercise your mind: play Scrabble, Sudoku, and crosswords, read novels, watch educational television. Expand your horizons: travel, join new groups, keep on learning. Relax regularly: sleep when you need to, watch a film, listen to music. Eat healthily: plenty of fresh fruit and vegetables and as much natural food as possible. Stop poisoning your system with tobacco and excessive alcohol. Keep healthy: see your doctor about symptoms that persist and listen to the options offered if you need treatment, then make informed decisions about what to have done. Be a mentor to those of a younger generation: let others benefit from your experiences while at the same time recognizing that the world is a different place from when you were their age, and so accept that their way of dealing with life may be different from yours.

Becoming 70 is a chance to open new doors and enjoy life to the fullest in whatever way you want. So recognize with gratitude that you are able to have opportunities to make a difference both in your own life and in the lives of those around you. Not only will you enjoy these years as you get older, but you will also leave behind a positive legacy.

23

Simple Steps to Downsize Your Home When You Turn 70

by Vickie Dellaquila

Vickie Dellaquila, Certified Professional Organizer and owner of Organization Rules, Inc., provides "compassionate organizing services for every stage of your life." She specializes in working with the chronically disorganized, seniors who are downsizing and moving, and those who hoard. Dellaquila is a member of the National Association of Professional Organizers; the National Association of Senior Move Managers; and the Institute for Challenging Disorganization, as western Pennsylvania's only Certified Professional Organizer in Chronic Disorganization. She is the author of *Don't Toss My Memories in the Trash: A Step-by-Step Guide to Helping Seniors Downsize, Organize, and Move.* For more information, visit organizationrules.com.

Jim and Marla lived in their beautiful two-story home for 38 years. It was once filled with their growing children and the neighborhood kids; now it seems quiet and empty. They used to be able to race up the stairs, but now the staircase has become difficult to manage. Their adult children worry about their safety. The house is too big and requires too much work. Recognizing that it is time to live in a more manageable space, they have decided to downsize and move to a smaller home. But how do they begin to consolidate 38 years' worth of stuff?

Like Jim and Marla, many seniors have a two-story, four- or five-bedroom home with several decades of dishes, furniture, slides, collections, and adult children's old term papers and toys. They know that all of these things are not going to fit in their new home, but sorting through their many possessions feels daunting. If you are starting the process of downsizing and moving on, consider these points:

- A good way to begin is to get someone to help you through the downsizing process, because it can be overwhelming. You'll be glad to have the physical assistance and the emotional support.

- Think about what items you really need and will definitely use. Do you still need place settings for 12, or will 6 be enough? If you always go to your son's home for Thanksgiving, do you really need a turkey roaster?

- Consider giving pieces of furniture or other items to family members or friends who have admired them for years. If your granddaughter has always loved your set of china, why not give it to her now, and see the happiness that it brings her?

- Adult children need to get their stuff out of your attic or spare bedroom! Unless you have decided to go into the storage business, your adult children must clear out their belongings.

- Do not overexert yourself. Start with small steps. Work a little each day on a section of your home, perhaps a drawer or a closet shelf.

- If you feel exhausted looking at a pile of papers that must be sorted, don't try to tackle it all at once. Set a timer for 15 minutes, start at the top of the pile, and then stop working when the timer goes off. You will make some progress and can continue the next day. Before you know it, you will have sorted through mountains of papers!

- Remember that every item you own requires your time, energy, maintenance, and money. Decide if the item is worth keeping.

- Look into charities and antique dealers that you can contact about donating or selling your unwanted possessions, and begin researching real estate agents and movers.

Downsizing can be emotionally and physically over-whelming, but you can make the process a little easier by taking things one step at a time and enlisting some assistance. With planning and organization, you can achieve a successful and happy transition.

24

Supercharge Activities You Already Do

by Peter Spiers

Peter Spiers is senior vice president at the nonprofit educational-travel organization Road Scholar, and he is the author of *Master Class: Living Longer, Stronger, and Happier* (Center Street, 2012). He is a graduate of Harvard College and the Tuck School of Business at Dartmouth. Spiers lives in Lexington, Massachusetts, with his wife, Melissa, and sons Tom and Andy.

For my book, *Master Class*, I interviewed hundreds of people who are aging successfully, and they convinced me that their secret for doing well was filling their lives with activities rich in four elements: socializing, physical activity, creativity, and thinking.

These "masters" also demonstrated a genius for finding ways to implement these elements by taking common pursuits and making them into "supercharged activities." Here are some of my favorite examples:

A book club on steroids — If you're not in a book club, you should consider joining one. You'll read more attentively, spend meaningful time with friends, and enjoy a glass of wine and a nibble of cheese. If you are in a book club, try this twist: instead of reading a book this month, choose a one-act play, assign parts, and read it aloud as a group. You'll interact with club members in a new way, you'll know the play more richly as you hear as well as read the words, and you may experience the drama through the eyes of a character of another gender, nationality, or race. Who knows? You might enjoy it so much that you'll try out for a role in community theater!

Volunteer and get a "grad school" education — Volunteering is good for society and the soul, but volunteering as a docent is also good for the body and brain. For *Master Class*, I spoke with docents in museums as far-flung and different from each other as Honolulu's Bishop Museum, the Oregon Coast Aquarium, and Harvard's Fogg Museum. These docents help museum visitors understand exhibits in new ways, get great exercise as they lead groups through exhibits, and stimulate their brains. Docents go through intense training to prepare them to think on their feet, answering questions from both wide-eyed children and knowledgeable adults. Contact museums and other cultural organizations near you — including public broadcasters — and ask if they're looking for new recruits.

Explore your own backyard with "new" eyes — Everyone loves to travel, but few can afford the time or money to travel as often or as far as they would like. Luckily, the benefits of travel can be had close to home. My interviews with intrepid local explorers led me to a simple exercise: find a map of your region and draw a circle 100 miles around your home. (This is about the distance you can drive in two hours.) Scrutinize the map closely, noting destinations you might have overlooked, then get online and learn what they have to offer. I live in Massachusetts, and this exercise led me to Hartford, Connecticut, a city I've driven through often but never thought of as more than a collection of insurance company buildings. (Was I ever wrong!) Hartford is the home of one of America's great smaller art museums, the Wadsworth Atheneum; two fascinating historical homes, the Mark Twain and Harriet Beecher Stowe houses; and the Hartford Stage, one of America's finest resident theaters. I'm planning a weekend there, and it's sure to be a rich experience.

Think about how you can spice another activity you already do with a little extra socializing, moving, creating, or thinking. Your retirement will be richer for it!

25

A Creative Sandwich

by Sheila Weinstein

Sheila Weinstein is a New York City writer and pianist. In 1991, she gave up teaching piano to pursue a writing career. After her husband of 42 years, a practicing ophthalmologist, was diagnosed with dementia, she wrote *Moving to the Center of the Bed: The Artful Creation of a Life Alone*, chronicling the years of his decline and her search for a new life without the love of her life. She adapted her book into a play. Weinstein is a docent at Carnegie Hall, where she performed in a 2008 concert in Weill Recital Hall. Please visit centerofthebed.com.

When I turned 20, I couldn't drink legally or vote, but I could marry, and I did. At 30, I was the mother of three. At 40, realizing I'd probably arrived at the halfway mark, I took to my bed after the birthday cake. Successive decades brought joys and sorrows. In my 60s, my husband, a practicing physician, was diagnosed with dementia. It took eight years for the disease to run its course.

I moved to New York City alone, feeling frightened and lonely. What has helped me through the sorrow and bewilderment of losing the man I loved all my life is my passion for music and writing. Depression has brought me the gift of songs. I've written 11 of them thus far. I became a docent at Carnegie Hall, taking visitors from all over the world on weekly tours. And, due to serendipitous circumstances, I played the piano there one glorious night. I wrote a book about learning to live alone after 42 years of marriage. At 75, I turned the book into a play, soon to be produced.

To be engaged in something joyful that takes me out of myself and yet into my deepest self continues to keep me alive and well.

The immutable facts are that, at this point in our lives, we are bound to lose connection with beloved friends and family, and we are more prone to illness. So to what can we turn for consolation and solace? I say: creativity, in any of its forms.

Those who create art can be elevated by it in spite of their circumstances and, in the process, touch other lives. Being open to others' creative works can also lift us above our personal pain. When I have a sad day, I go to a museum and sit in front of some of the grandest paintings ever created, knowing that those artists, too, were translating their pain, love, and loneliness into their work. It makes me feel connected to something grander than myself.

I define creativity broadly. At a book signing, I talked about the value of creativity to a group of women who were in various stages of grief. One woman stood and said, "Well, that's fine, but some of us are not creative." I asked her, "Can you make a sandwich?" She replied, "Of course!" I said, "Then make one (or two, or ten), put it in a bag with some other goodies, take it out on the street, and feed someone who's hungry. That's creative. It will nourish someone else — and you as well."

If you don't believe you are creative, simply seek ways to help others. Find the need and creatively fill it. Deliver an anonymous basket of food, or tape a little gift on the door of an aging neighbor. Offer to read to someone in a hospital. The possibilities are endless.

Whatever your interest, stay connected to it. You will be enriched.

I wish you a healthy and creative life!

26

Beginning My First Novel — at 70!

by Beverly Scott

Bev Scott is currently focused on writing her first novel, based on the story of her paternal grandparents. She also writes about the issues and challenges of the boomer and older generations. Scott is the founder and creator of The 3rd Act, whose mission is to support positive aging. She has served as an internal organization-and-management consultant for over 35 years, taught organizational psychology, established an independent consulting and coaching practice, and published the second edition of *Consulting on the Inside*, which she coauthored with Kim Barnes in 2011. Scott is now in what she considers to be scene 3 of her own third act, and she enjoys creating and writing the script.

"What an intriguing story. You should write a book about it." This was the common response from friends and acquaintances as I related my discoveries of my paternal grandparents' story, after doing genealogical research at the National Archives in Washington more than 25 years ago. Although I heard this encouragement repeated over the ensuing years, I was too focused on my career and other professional projects to make time to write a book.

As I approached my 70th birthday, I began to reflect more on what goals and aspirations I had not yet pursued. At the top of my "bucket list" was writing my family story. I had uncovered some juicy tidbits about my grandparents, such as the secret my grandfather kept from my grandmother — that he had abandoned his first wife and their six children without bothering to get a divorce before remarrying. Yet, there was still so much I didn't know about their background history and personal motivations that I wondered if the only way to tell their story was as a work of fiction, using the facts of their lives as the framework for what would ultimately be a novel. That is when I came face-to-face with my anxiety. Could I even write fiction? A novel! At my age! It seemed pretty preposterous.

I had authored three nonfiction professional books and numerous articles, but I had never written — let alone published — either short stories or a novel. I decided

I needed to find out more about what was required, and so I took two workshops. I learned a lot, including that it is important for an author to know as much as possible about the specific details and atmosphere of a setting before writing about it.

I took off with my partner on a long road trip through New Mexico, Oklahoma, Kansas, Nebraska, and Wyoming to visit the significant locations where my grandparents lived. It was quite an odyssey, searching for my grandfather's grave, visiting museums, discovering the surprising fact that at one time my grandparents probably lived in a dugout (a shelter carved out of the ground, often in places where lumber was scarce), finding resources in libraries, and going to a small historical museum in Nebraska and chancing upon a book about my family that had been compiled by a distant relative. But I didn't uncover any information to close the gaps of my grandparents' personal story. So, that settled it. I realized I would need to write a fictionalized account of their lives.

As my 70th birthday arrived, I had a plan. I took the bittersweet step of leaving a project I had founded, called The 3rd Act, which promotes positive aging for those of us over 55. I joined a writing group, took more workshops, read other writers' work, and attended a writer's conference. Finally, I set about writing the novel. I love the creativity of the process and all the learning I get to do! I am having a good time working on the story, depicting the setting, and developing my characters. I am excited to be launched on this new adventure, and I anticipate completing the first draft of my novel for my next birthday!

27

Never Too Late

by Julie Kertesz, Ph.D.

Julie Kertesz, Ph.D., from Paris, is of Hungarian origin and celebrates her 77 years of age as she celebrates life itself. She is retired from her careers as a research chemist (in Paris and Washington, D.C.) and as the founder of a computer-products distribution company in Paris. Kertesz now defines herself as a storyteller, a photographer, a prolific blogger, a keynote speaker, a coach, and, finally, as a stand-up comedian. She won the title "Silver Comedy Newcomer 2012," and she is popular with audiences everywhere she appears. Her blog is at competentcommunicator.blogspot.com.

At age 40, I protested: I am not too old to dance! At 50, in love again, I proved it. At 60, I realized with joy I was the youngest member of my Retired Teachers Association. Arriving at 70, I had to admit finally: I am a senior.

Three months before my 70th birthday, I began learning photography and strolled Paris streets with my camera.

There *is* life after 70! To prove to myself and all others that this is true, I started a blog, in French (*Il y a de la vie après 70 ans*). I have been writing every morning now for nine years.

Desiring a special treat to remember my 70th birthday, I went on a trip and realized to my delight that I could still drive long hours if I needed to, even alone. I met an old flame and . . . yes! . . . we still could . . . ! One is never really too old for that! We still feel young inside.

At 74, I moved with my son's family from Paris to London. I joined a Toastmasters club to improve my public speaking skills, to meet people, and to relate stories from my life. A year later, I was able to tell my true stories, in a theater. Me, of Hungarian mother language, after 40 years in France, storytelling live in English!

To my surprise, when I was 77 I discovered, learned, and began to practice stand-up comedy. What a joy! I had a funny bone, after all — I only had to cultivate it. From then on, I began to look at all my life's frustrations, even my cataract operations, with a comedian's eye. Life seems so much easier now. And full.

After performing 60+ comedy gigs at different clubs

and having a marvelous connection with my audiences, I can affirm now, at almost 80, that we can be as creative as before — or even more so — use all we have . . . and even what we don't have any more.

I use my age's joys and frustrations in my stories and also in my comedy set. First, by recognizing what the audience sees — my age — and wondering out loud, "What is she doing here?" Then, instead of just telling them, I show them that, in essence, I am no different from them. When I mock the experiences and problems I have at my age, we all laugh together. For example, one of the things I tell them is:

> . . . We women indeed have a great advantage over men. I always thought: we do not have to shave every day. (*Pause.*) That is, until we get to 50. Then, the first hairs began to grow here and there, so I plucked them out fast. They grew back. I photoshopped them out. That worked. But only on the screen alas.

We can dare, experiment, and learn as we did when we were children. After 70, we are even less shy to do it: using fully the time left to us . . . and enjoying it. Yes, we can. It is never too late.

28

Engage Musically and Create the Life You Want to Live

by Ed Merck

Ed Merck spent 30 rewarding years as chief financial officer and/or a member of the music faculty at several prestigious universities and colleges. Subsequently, assuming the role of business entrepreneur, he codeveloped Future Perfect, the premier strategic/financial modeling tool used in higher education today. In recent years, Merck has gravitated toward pursuits of the heart — writing, making music, teaching yoga, sailing the East Coast of America, and offering workshops in "Conscious Aging." He is the author of the recently published book *Sailing the Mystery: My Journey into Life's Remaining Chapters.* Merck currently resides on Martha's Vineyard, Massachusetts, and can be reached at sailingthemystery.com.

"Oh Ed, I never saw this part of you; I never felt your heart," Marilyn, my longtime secretary, said to me after the concert, as tears streamed down her cheeks.

Toward the end of my career as an overly left-brained chief financial officer — a type A on steroids — an opportunity to reclaim my musical past emerged. The invitation came from an acclaimed harpsichordist, who was the chair of the music department at the college where I worked as the VP for Finance and Operations. His request — challenge, really — was to dust off my flutes after many years of inactivity, and join him in a performance of Baroque sonatas. Marilyn's tears that day, after years of a distant, often strained relationship between us, were a poignant message: now is the time to begin recovering your right brain, the more creative, heart-centered essence of who you are, and to better integrate all the parts, so you can feel more whole.

That was the wake-up call. Now, just a hair's distance from the 70-year-old milestone, I have intensified my engagement in musical activities of all types — traditional playing, deep listening, and even free improvisation. What I learned about balance from Marilyn's surprise tears has held me in good stead. And I've noticed that the older I get, the better able I am to access my own creativity. As a bonus, I have learned that music can help me reconcile many of the challenges of aging, by shifting my focus from capacities that are diminishing to those that are expanding.

Keeping up with the whirl of technological advances, which left me in the dust several years ago, is not a game I wish to engage in. Leave that to the "digital natives" of the younger generation, I say to myself, those whose beta-wave-oriented brains are in full-flourish mode. Instead, I want to explore the new territory that is emerging: the glory of slowing down and becoming more mindful. *Bequeath the left-brain razzle-dazzle to the young turks*, says the voice within, *and explore instead what is now available — a life of greater spaciousness.*

One of the beauties of music as an activity is its accessibility. It is never too late to start, and the entry-level requirements are minimal — just a willingness to cross the threshold into a world of awakened senses. Our bodies deteriorate year after year, and our brains tire of rapid-fire calculations. Meanwhile, our spirits begin to crave expansiveness, and our minds gravitate toward slower, yet deeper, immersions. Why not go with what is opening to us, rather than what is falling away?

For me, engaging in music changes my experience of aging, from a sense of loss to a sense of gain. It allows me to encounter the remaining chapters of my life as an act of grace — a major leap forward in my expanding capacity as a loving, spiritual being.

29

Excerpt from *At Seventy: A Journal*

by May Sarton

May Sarton is the pen name of Eleanore Marie Sarton (May 3, 1912–July 16, 1995), an American poet, novelist, and memoirist. Her parents were science historian George Sarton and his wife, the English artist Mabel Eleanor Elwes. In 1915, her family moved to Boston, Massachusetts. She went to school in Cambridge, Massachusetts, and started theater lessons in her late teens. In 1945, she met her partner for the next 13 years, Judy Matlack, in Santa Fe, New Mexico. They separated in 1956, when Sarton's father died and Sarton moved to Nelson, New Hampshire. *Honey in the* Hive (1988) is about their relationship. Sarton later moved to York, Maine. She died of breast cancer on July 16, 1995. She is buried in Nelson, New Hampshire.

What is it like to be seventy? If someone else had lived so long and could remember things sixty years ago with great clarity, she would seem very old to me. But I do not feel old at all, not as much a survivor as a person still on her way. I suppose real old age begins when one looks backward rather than forward, but I look forward with joy to the years ahead and especially to the surprises that any day may bring.

In the middle of the night things well up from the past that are not always cause for rejoicing — the unsolved, the painful encounters, the mistakes, the reasons for shame or woe. But all, good or bad, painful or delightful, weave themselves into a rich tapestry, and all give me food for thought, food to grow on.

I am just back from a month of poetry readings, in and out through all of April. At Hartford College in Connecticut I had been asked to talk about old age — "The View From Here," I called the reading — in a series on "The Seasons of Womanhood." In the course of it I said, "This is the best time of my life. I love being old." At that point a voice from the audience asked loudly, "Why is it good to be old?" I answered spontaneously and a little on the defensive, for I sensed incredulity in the questioner, "Because I am more myself than I have ever been. There is less conflict. I am happier, more balanced, and" (I heard myself say rather aggressively) "more powerful." I felt it was rather an odd word, "powerful," but I think it is true. It might have been more accurate to say, "I am better able to use my powers." I am surer of what my life is all about, have less self-doubt to conquer, although it has to be admitted that I wrote my new novel *Anger* in an agony of self-doubt most of the year, the hardest subject I have attempted to deal with in a novel since *Mrs. Stevens Hears the Mermaids Singing*. There I was breaking new ground, giving myself away. I was fifty-three and I deliberately made Mrs. Stevens seventy, and now here I am at what then seemed eons away, safely "old."

Mark Twain's Seventieth Birthday Address

at a dinner given by Colonel George Harvey at Delmonico's, New York, December 5, 1905

by Mark Twain

Mark Twain (1835–1910) was a humorist and philosopher whose novels, stories, essays, and speeches are among the most beloved and enduring works of American literature ever published.

I have had a great many birthdays in my time. I remember the first one very well, and I always think of it with indignation; everything was so crude, unaesthetic, primeval. Nothing like this at all. No proper appreciative preparation made; nothing really ready. Now, for a person born with high and delicate

Publisher's note: This famous speech is reprinted with most of the original punctuation intact.

instincts — why, even the cradle wasn't whitewashed — nothing ready at all. I hadn't any hair, I hadn't any teeth, I hadn't any clothes, I had to go to my first banquet just like that. Well, everybody came swarming in. It was the merest little bit of a village — hardly that, just a little hamlet, in the backwoods of Missouri, where nothing ever happened, and the people were all interested, and they all came; they looked me over to see if there was anything fresh in my line. Why, nothing ever happened in that village — I — why, I was the only thing that had really happened there for months and months and months; And although I say it myself that shouldn't, I came the nearest to being a real event that had happened in that village in more than two years. Well, those people came, they came with that curiosity which is so provincial with that frankness, which also is so provincial, and they examined me all around and gave their opinion. Nobody asked them, and I shouldn't have minded if anybody had paid me a compliment, but nobody did. Their opinions were all just green with prejudice, and I feel those opinions to this day. Well, I stood that as long as — well, you know I was born courteous and I stood it to the limit. I stood it an hour, and then the worm turned. I was the worm; it was my turn to turn, and I turned. I knew very well the strength of my position; I knew that I was the only spotlessly pure and innocent person in that whole town, and I came out and said so. And they could not say a word. It was so true. They blushed; they were embarrassed. Well that was the first after-dinner speech I ever made. I think it was after dinner.

It's a long stretch between that first birthday speech and this one. That was my cradle-song, and this is my swan-song, I suppose. I am used to swan-songs; I have sung them several times.

This is my seventieth birthday, and I wonder if you all rise to the size of that proposition, realizing all the significance of that phrase, seventieth birthday.

The seventieth birthday! It is the time of life when you arrive at a new and awful dignity; when you may throw aside the decent reserves which have oppressed you for a generation and stand unafraid and unabashed upon your seven-terraced summit and look down and teach — unrebuked. You can tell the world how you got there. It is what they all do. You shall never get tired of telling by what delicate arts and deep moralities you climbed up to that great place. You will explain the process and dwell on the particulars with senile rapture. I have been anxious to explain my own system this long time, and now at last I have the right.

I have achieved my seventy years in the usual way: by sticking strictly to a scheme of life which would kill anybody else. It sounds like an exaggeration, but that is really the common rule for attaining to old age. When we examine the programme of any of these garrulous old people we always find that the habits which have preserved them would have decayed us; that the way of life which enabled them to live upon the property of their heirs so long, as Mr. Choate says, would have put us out of commission ahead of time. I will offer here, as a sound maxim, this: That we can't reach old age by another man's road.

I will now teach, offering my way of life to whomsoever desires to commit suicide by the scheme which has enabled me to beat the doctor and the hangman for seventy years. Some of the details may sound untrue, but they are not. I am not here to deceive; I am here to teach.

We have no permanent habits until we are forty. Then they begin to harden, presently they petrify, then business begins. Since forty I have been regular about going to bed and getting up — and that is one of the main things. I have made it a rule to go to bed when there wasn't anybody left to sit up with; and I have made it a rule to get up when I had to. This has resulted in an unswerving regularity of irregularity. It has saved me sound, but it would injure another person.

In the matter of diet — which is another main thing — I have been persistently strict in sticking to the things which didn't agree with me until one or the other of us got the best of it. Until lately I got the best of it myself. But last spring I stopped frolicking with mince-pie after midnight; up to then I had always believed it wasn't loaded. For thirty years I have taken coffee and bread at eight in the morning, and no bite nor sup until seven-thirty in the evening. Eleven hours. That is all right for me, and is wholesome, because I have never had a headache in my life, but headachy people would not reach seventy comfortably by that road, and they would be foolish to try it. And I wish to urge upon you this — which I think is wisdom — that if you find you can't make seventy by any but an uncomfortable road, don't you go. When they take off the Pullman and retire you to the rancid smoker, put on your things, count your checks, and get out at the first way station where there's a cemetery.

I have made it a rule never to smoke more than one cigar at a time. I have no other restriction as regards smoking. I do not know just when I began to smoke, I only know that it was in my father's lifetime, and that I was discreet. He passed from this life early in 1847, when I was a shade past eleven; ever since then I have smoked publicly. As an example to others, and not that I care for moderation myself, it has always been my rule never to smoke when asleep, and never to refrain when awake. It is a good rule. I mean, for me; but some of you know quite well that it wouldn't answer for everybody that's trying to get to be seventy.

I smoke in bed until I have to go to sleep; I wake up in the night, sometimes once, sometimes twice, sometimes three times, and I never waste any of these opportunities to smoke. This habit is so old and dear and precious to me that I would feel as you, sir, would feel if you should lose the only moral you've got — meaning the chairman — if you've got one: I am making no charges. I will grant, here, that I have stopped smoking now and then, for a few months at a time, but it was not on principle, it was only to show off; it was to pulverize those critics who said I was a slave to my habits and couldn't break my bonds.

To-day it is all of sixty years since I began to smoke the limit. I have never bought cigars with life-belts around them. I early found that those were too expensive for me. I have always bought cheap cigars — reasonably cheap, at any rate. Sixty years ago they cost me four dollars a barrel, but my taste has improved, latterly, and I pay seven now. Six or seven. Seven, I think. Yes, it's seven. But that includes the barrel. I often have smoking-parties at my house; but the people that come have always just taken the pledge. I wonder why that is?

As for drinking, I have no rule about that. When the others drink I like to help; otherwise I remain dry, by habit and preference. This dryness does not hurt me, but it could easily hurt you, because you are different. You let it alone.

Since I was seven years old I have seldom taken a dose of medicine, and have still seldomer needed one. But up to seven I lived exclusively on allopathic medicines. Not that I needed them, for I don't think I did; it was for economy; my father took a drug-store for a debt, and it made cod-liver oil cheaper than the other breakfast foods. We had nine barrels of it, and it lasted me seven years. Then. I was weaned. The rest of the family had to get along with rhubarb and ipecac and such things, because I was the pet. I was the first Standard Oil Trust. I had it all. By the time the drug store was exhausted my health was established, and there has never been much the matter with me since. But you know very well it would be foolish for the average child to start for seventy on that basis. It happened to be just the thing for me, but that was merely an accident; it couldn't happen again in a century.

I have never taken any exercise, except sleeping and resting, and I never intend to take any. Exercise is loathsome. And it cannot be any benefit when you are tired; and I was always tired. But let another person try my way, and see where he will come out.

I desire now to repeat and emphasize that maxim: We can't reach old age by another man's road. My habits protect my life, but they would assassinate you.

I have lived a severely moral life. But it would be a mistake for other people to try that, or for me to recommend it. Very few would succeed: you have to have a perfectly colossal stock of morals; and you can't get them on a margin; you have to have the whole thing, and put them in your box. Morals are an acquirement — like music, like a foreign language, like piety, poker, paralysis — no man is born with them. I wasn't myself, I started poor. I hadn't a single moral. There is hardly a man in this house that is poorer than I was then. Yes, I started like that — the world before me, not a moral in the slot. Not even an insurance moral. I can remember the first one I ever got. I can remember the landscape, the weather, the — I can remember how everything looked. It was an old moral, an old second-hand moral, all out of repair, and didn't fit, anyway. But if you are careful with a thing like that, and keep it in a dry place, and save it for processions, and Chautauquas, and World's Fairs, and so on, and disinfect it now and then, and give it a fresh coat of whitewash once in a while, you will be surprised to see how well she will last and how long she will keep sweet, or at least inoffensive. When I got that moldy old moral, she had stopped growing, because she hadn't any exercise; but I worked her hard, I worked her Sundays and all. Under this cultivation she waxed in might and stature beyond belief, and served me well and was my pride and joy for sixty-three years; then she got to associating with insurance presidents, and lost flesh and character, and was a sorrow to look at and no longer competent for business. She was a great loss to me. Yet not all loss. I sold her — ah, pathetic skeleton, as she was — I sold her to Leopold, the pirate King of Belgium; he sold her to our Metropolitan Museum, and it was very glad to get her, for without a rag on, she stands 57 feet long and 16 feet high, and they think she's a brontosaur. Well, she looks it. They believe it will take nineteen geological periods to breed her match.

Morals are of inestimable value, for every man is born crammed with sin microbes, and the only thing that can extirpate these sin microbes is morals. Now you take a sterilized Christian — I mean, you take the sterilized Christian, for there's only one. Dear sir, I wish you wouldn't look at me like that.

Threescore years and ten!

It is the Scriptural statute of limitations. After that, you owe no active duties; for you the strenuous life is over. You are a time-expired man, to use Kipling's military phrase: You have served your term, well or less well, and you are mustered out. You are become an honorary member of the republic, you are emancipated, compulsions are not for you, not any bugle-call but "lights out." You pay the time-worn duty bills if you choose, or decline if you prefer — and without prejudice — for they are not legally collectable.

The previous-engagement plea, which in forty years has cost you so many twinges, you can lay aside forever; on this side of the grave you will never need it again. If you shrink at the thought of night and winter, and the late home-coming from the banquet and the lights and the laughter through the deserted streets — a desolation which would not remind you now, as for a generation it did, that your friends are sleeping, and you must creep in a-tiptoe and not disturb them, but would only remind you that you need not tiptoe, you can never disturb them more — if you shrink at thought of these things, you need only reply, "Your invitation honors me, and pleases me because you still keep me in your remembrance, but I am seventy; seventy, and would nestle in the chimney-corner, and smoke my pipe, and read my book, and take my rest, wishing you well in all affection, and that when you in your return shall arrive at pier No. 70 you may step aboard your waiting ship with a reconciled spirit, and lay your course toward the sinking sun with a contented heart."

31

At Seventy

by Judith Viorst

Judith Viorst was born and brought up in New Jersey, graduated from Rutgers University, moved to Greenwich Village, and has lived in Washington, D.C., since 1960, when she married Milton Viorst, a political writer. They have three sons and seven grandchildren. Viorst writes in many different areas: science books, children's picture books, adult fiction and nonfiction, poetry for children and adults, and musicals, which are still performed on stages around the country. She is best known for her beloved picture book *Alexander and the Terrible, Horrible, No Good, Very Bad Day*.

Instead of "old,"

Let us consider

"Older,"

Or maybe "oldish,"

Or something, anything,

That isn't always dressed

In sensible shoes

And fading underwear.

Besides which,

Seventy isn't old.

Ninety is old.

And though eighty

Is probably old,

We needn't decide that

Until we get there.

In the meantime

Let us consider

Drinking wine,

Making love,

Laughing hard,

Caring hard,

And learning a new trick or two

As part of our job description

At seventy.

Part

2

KEEPING ACTIVE
AND CARING FOR
YOUR BODY

32

Fitness First

by Caroline Anaya

Author Caroline Anaya holds a B.S. and M.S. in foods and nutrition. She spent most of her professional life in research, teaching, and consulting. Her passion for fitness spawned her popular book, *The Curious Upside of Growing Older: And the 7 Keys That Active Seniors Embrace for the Best Life, Including the Best Food, Exercise, Sleep and Memory*. She has also created her Web site at great-senior-fitness.com to help people get started, as well as DVDs and the *Fit Bits* e-newsletter, which features timely news about body and brain fitness. Healthy and happy at 80 years old, Anaya teaches classes, writes, and is raising her grandson.

I n my 60s, the vague notion entered my awareness that I was getting older . . . for real. There were hints: AARP came calling, I was offered free coffee at McDonald's, and I received brochures for financial planning and long-term care, discounts on cemetery plots, and last-chance life insurance.

It was unnerving.

I decided to just ignore all of that "information" and simply live each day as though I were having a great life.

Of course, having a "great life" depends on the person . . . but it's intuitively obvious that to have a great life, one must be healthy. To be healthy, one must cultivate a fit body and mind.

How? You can start by following the seven keys that active seniors embrace in order to live the best life possible:

1. **Know yourself.** Take a fearless self-assessment. It's a lot easier now than when you were in your 50s and spent time reading books, going to seminars, and trying to find your "true calling." As you reach your 70s, you'll have greater clarity about your journey . . . as if you are looking down from above, seeing the whole picture. You'll see the path you've been on, and can extrapolate from that how to move forward.

2. **Think healthy — be healthy.** What you think becomes your words; your words become your actions; your actions become your destiny.

3. **Eat healthy.** It's not that easy anymore. Eat light.

Eat fresh. Eat organic. Eat local. Eat natural. Do not eat processed foods.

4. **Sleep well.** Your body needs to rest and recharge itself. Use natural remedies for sleeplessness.

5. **Exercise.** Find a fitness program that suits you. Just ask around. Visit gyms, community centers, and YMCAs. I know, you're probably nervous, but be brave. You may find yourself making new friends right away. Take an exercise class, dance, swim, play Ping-Pong, whatever! Just get active, five to six days a week. I know from experience that everybody can exercise in one way or another. Soon, you'll feel so much better . . . especially if you stretch or do yoga as part of your routine.

6. **Work your brain.** Think about this: your brain changes due to your experiences, and then your next experience is different due to your recently changed brain. So, have a new experience: learn a language, join a choir, mentor a child, start a business. And no, crossword puzzles just don't do the trick.

7. **Socialize.** Get out of the house. Make new friends. Join social groups and clubs. Go places. Do stuff. Have some fun.

***

There you have it — seven keys for achieving the pinnacle of good health. Tried and true. They worked for me. They will work for you, too.

So, when you turn 70 . . . CELEBRATE . . . because you've already made many wise choices in your life, or you wouldn't have made it this far. Then, lay the foundation to make the years ahead the best they can be by cultivating fitness first . . . and stay with it always.

When you have good health, all else follows easily.

33

Enjoy Tai Chi — on Either Side of 70

by Master Domingo Colon

Domingo Colon started on his Tai Chi path at age 15. In 1978, he was honored to receive the "Master" designation from Grand Master C. K. Chu of the Tai Chi Center. After more than 47 years of Tai Chi experience, he was given the prestigious *Action Martial Arts* magazine "Hall of Honors 2013 Excellence in Teaching of Martial Arts" award. Master Colon uses his physical-therapy training and understanding of anatomy, physiology, and kinesiology to enhance his practice and promotion of Tai Chi. He created the Teaching Tai Chi to Special Populations program and wrote *Senior's Tai Chi Workout*, both of which focus on adapting Tai Chi so that anyone may benefit from this profound, ancient health system. Learn more at taichischool.com.

Moving softly, gracefully, and being fully balanced . . . does this sound good to you? Then start Tai Chi lessons now — whether you are about to turn 70 or you passed this milestone years ago! Anyone can benefit from the increased body awareness, improved breathing and circulation, stronger muscles and bones, and better flexibility that Tai Chi gives you.

You may have seen Tai Chi before, perhaps in a movie or a TV documentary about China, without realizing that you were looking at the most popular exercise and health program in the world. Picture the scene: groups of mature Chinese performing smooth, flowing movements in a park or plaza, all with peaceful looks on their faces. That's Tai Chi!

With its slow, gentle, and fluid motions, Tai Chi has an almost dance-like nature. The quality of these movements is very different from other forms of exercise, which push the practitioner to work harder for various benefits, like cardio development or weight loss. But in Tai Chi, you want to relax and release the tension that interferes with the normal movements and function of your body.

The unique approach and style of practicing Tai Chi stimulates the so-called "relaxation response." This response is basically the opposite of the stress reaction generated by more rigorous forms of exercise, which we now know can either cause or exacerbate many health problems. With Tai Chi, blood pressure usually goes down, and the pulse rate slows; breathing becomes deeper; and the practitioner feels thoroughly relaxed and at peace.

Let's try a simple Tai Chi move and feel what it's really like:

Either seated or standing, place your hands in front of your body as if holding a ball — say, a very light beach ball — from top and bottom. Keep your hands gently curved to follow the surface of the ball. Feel your shoulders become relaxed and loose as your elbows drop gently. Now, slowly turn your waist to one side, bringing the ball to your side, then imagine rolling the ball over so that you reverse your hand position. Then turn your waist to the other side, bringing the ball to your opposite side. When you finish turning, continue rolling the ball, reversing your hand placement and moving the ball from one side to the other.

Keep turning from side to side while rolling the ball over. Feel your arms become lighter and softer as you breathe slowly and deeply. Notice how you are becoming more and more relaxed with each repetition. Repeat as many times as you like, enjoying the freedom from stress and tension in your upper body.

There! That's a beginning movement of Tai Chi. Not so difficult, right? Of course, there are many movements, some which are rather complex and require precise guidance from an instructor, but now you have a feel for what Tai Chi is like. Don't you think this is something you should explore? Whatever your age, you can enjoy the benefits of Tai Chi for many years to come.

34

Learn to Squat!

by Edna Levitt

Edna Levitt, a certified personal trainer, was trained and certified by the Certified Professional Trainers Network in Toronto. She launched 50+ Fitness in 2006, focusing exclusively on muscle toning, strength building, and enhanced physical performance for people in her own age group, 50+. In addition to personal training, Levitt teaches fitness at Better Living Health and Community Services in Toronto, and she has presented her seminar, "Muscles Matter — The Benefits of Strength Training" to CARP chapters and seniors' organizations throughout southern Ontario. At age 70, Levitt published her exercise book, *Personal Trainer to Go*. Her Web site is at 50plus-fitness.ca.

I'm not kidding. One definition of squat is "hunker down," and I'm suggesting that squatting is definitely one of the things to do when you turn 70.

May I step back a bit before I continue?

When I turned 65, I felt that it was time I tried something new. On an impulse, I enrolled in a course to become a personal trainer, a program exclusively for "vintage" adults. I had only started exercising when I turned 50, and when I saw the difference it made to my mind and body, I thought that I should "spread the word." I was determined to convince the 65+ population that exercising in general, and squatting in particular, would do amazing things for their mobility.

Why squatting? The bad news is that, as we age, we lose a small percentage of muscle mass each year, and as these years add up, we lose overall strength and endurance. The good news is that we can reverse this loss by strength training, and that is what I advocate to my clients, who are mostly over 70.

Here's what you should do. Every morning when you're in the kitchen, waiting for the kettle to boil or the coffee to brew, rest your hands lightly on the countertop, stand about 18 inches away, and do the following:

Stand straight with your shoulders back, suck in your tummy, and stand with your feet shoulder-width apart. Bend at the knees and reach back with your butt as if you're sitting in a chair. Stop when your hips are knee level (do not allow your knees to extend past your toes as you lower down). Exhale and s-q-u-e-e-z-e your butt and your abdominals as you press yourself back to a standing position.

There! Was that difficult?

Repeat three sets of 12 squats every morning. I promise you that it's only going to take about one and a half minutes (bet you thought it would take much longer!). Squatting uses several large muscle groups (quads, glutes, and hamstrings) and works your hip joints, so there are definite benefits — maybe the most important is that your quad (thigh) muscles are the ones that get you up from the toilet! And you're using your quad muscles continuously while squatting.

Here are a few more ideas for working those muscles. (You'll thank me, I promise you.) While watching the television, sit forward on your chair, keep your back straight, straighten one leg, and raise it 12 to 18 inches off the floor, with your foot flexed. Do this exercise 12 times, switch legs, and repeat 12 times. Do this twice more (72 lifts in total). Another great exercise for the glutes is to sit forward on your chair, with your heels firmly on the floor, and s-q-u-e-e-z-e your butt 40 times, continuously.

If you do these every day, it won't be long before you notice a difference, and you'll never need help getting up from a chair — or the toilet!

35

Do It! The Importance of Fitness

by Esther and Martin Kafer

Esther and Martin Kafer were both born and raised in Zurich, Switzerland. They immigrated to Canada in 1954, working first in Quebec and then raising a son and a daughter in Vancouver, close to the mountains and the wilderness. In British Columbia, they were able to indulge in their long-standing passion for mountaineering and skiing. They have now hiked or climbed hundreds of mountains on most continents. Some of their "peak experiences" include the Matterhorn on their honeymoon and, in 2012, a world-record hike to the top of Mt. Kilimanjaro to benefit the British Columbia Alzheimer's Society.

We, Esther and Martin, have a cherished mantra: "Every day after 70 is a BONUS DAY." Enjoy each day to the fullest!

To reach a happy old age, you must remain fit: mentally, physically, and socially. Here are these three fitness spheres, as well as some of the things we have done since turning 70:

Keep fit mentally. Every day, engage in challenging mental activities. Read books and the newspaper, write a story, do crosswords, or play a mentally stimulating game like chess. See a movie or a play. Keep your mind fresh by learning something new.

In recent years, we have attended lectures and taken night-school courses in Spanish, Photoshop, life-writing, bridge, and oil painting. We practice public speaking at various venues and have season tickets to the theater.

Keep fit physically. Exercise regularly, whether it's tennis, swimming, going to the gym, hiking, or dancing — anything you choose, but DO IT!

We have always been enthusiastic nature lovers; now we hike two or three days most weeks, and in winter we spend two days downhill skiing and hiking an icy trail up Grouse Mountain, often accompanied by friends.

Our upper-body fitness has been improved by group canoe trips, where we enjoy the challenges of food planning, choosing camps, and judging the weather, tide, and river conditions.

Keep fit socially. Maintain contact with family members, but especially with friends. Volunteer or join a club to share activities with like-minded people.

We are members of the B.C. Mountaineering Club, a canoe club, and the Brock House Senior Centre. Our wide circle of friends and Esther's love of cooking result in many dinner parties at our home. We also have very close, loving contact with our two adult children.

We have found that traveling includes all three fitnesses. Almost every year, for six to eight weeks, we have visited exotic places in Africa, South America, and Asia, hiking up a hill, climbing a mountain, or backpacking whenever possible, which maintains our physical fitness.

Two recent trips involving charities also helped our mental and social fitness. In 2006, the Trans-Himalayan Aid Society (TRAS) organized a visit to remote northern India, where it supports a large residential school. We traveled from Delhi to Shimla (where the two of us bought 400 toothbrushes for the children), then truck-camped via Land Rover all the way to Spiti's Munsel-Ling school. The kids sang and a local

Lama prayed as we placed cornerstones for a TRAS-sponsored infirmary.

In 2012, as part of a team of 11, we hiked for seven strenuous days up 19,354-foot Mt. Kilimanjaro, raising over $25,000 for the Alzheimer Society of B.C. On top and at the camps, we were videotaped and photographed, because Esther (at 84) and Martin (at 85) are now in the Guinness World Records as the oldest woman and man to climb Mt. Kilimanjaro.

We hope that our experiences will inspire you to discover your own fitness activities after 70 — and that you, too, will make the most of all of these "bonus days."

36

Learn to Sail

by Steve Colgate

Steve Colgate has sailed from the age of 9 and is now 78. He raced six Transatlantic Races, the 1963 Pan American Games, the 1968 Olympics, two America's Cup trials, 20 Newport Bermuda Races, two Sydney to Hobart Yacht Races, seven Fastnet Races (including the infamous 1979 race, where 15 sailors died in a storm), and many other sailing venues all over the world. Colgate has written 13 books on sailing. He started Offshore Sailing School in 1964 and is one of the oldest members of the New York Yacht Club.

Sailing is so rewarding and easy to learn that there is never a time when you are too old. My wife, Doris, and I own Offshore Sailing School, which will turn 50 in 2014. We have eight locations, one of which is South Seas Island Resort on Captiva Island, Florida. There I met a 79-year-old woman who told me she was learning to sail because she thought it would be too late when she turned 80. Twelve years later, at 92, she took the course again to attain Basic Keelboat certification (and to impress her great-grandchildren when she took them sailing on Lake Michigan). She passed with flying colors!

Sailing keeps you active, whether you sail a small boat for a few hours at a time, purchase a larger sailboat to cruise near home, daysail and race with friends, or charter cruising yachts in exotic locales. Sailing gives you a true sense of profound freedom. It lets you relax as you enjoy the great outdoors and natural surroundings. Sailing also lets you bond with the younger generation unlike any other opportunity.

Since our profession for the past 50 years has been teaching the skills to take the helm, Doris and I have met incredible people of all ages on this journey. I am most inspired by the graduates who have crossed the 70 threshold. Just seeing their enjoyment, their desire to learn, and their love of adventure makes the experience more gratifying for all of us who teach them. Sailing is one of those therapeutic, eye-opening experiences that truly can be enjoyed at any stage of life.

At 78, I still love to race maxi-sailboats. But more and more, a favorite activity is to go cruising. A few months ago, Doris and I chartered a 54-foot sailboat in the

British Virgin Islands, and we laughed our way through a week of great sailing with another couple.

We have cruised the Greek Islands, Belize, St. Lucia to Grenada and back in the Caribbean, and other beautiful locales — all after the age of 70. I sailed in the 1968 Olympics with Dr. Stuart Walker, who is 92 years old now, and last summer he was second in the Soling European Championships as skipper. Stuart is the exception in that class, since the Soling is a very physical boat to sail, but he proves that sailing is for anyone of any age.

One of our recent graduates, Gary Firestone, wrote to us: "This was a bucket-list item for me! My recent retirement has allowed me to realize a dream that has been tucked away from the '60s, when I lived in the Midwest." If you're heading toward 70 or are already 70ish, add learning to sail to your "bucket list"!

37

Becoming a Free Spirit After 70

by Hazel Reynolds

Hazel Reynolds was born on October 14, 1933, in Corrine, West Virginia. After her father was seriously injured in a coal-mining accident, her family moved to her grandmother's farm in Christiansburg, Virginia, where she and her brothers attended a one-room schoolhouse and spent summers feeding the farm animals, churning butter, and picking berries. Her first job was with a finance company in Columbus, Ohio, and she retired from banking in 1989. A mother of three and a widow since 2000, Reynolds currently lives in Whitehall, Ohio, not far from her two beloved grandchildren.

I turned 70 three years after my husband died. As time went by, I felt like I was stuck in a rut, and I knew I had to do something to change my life. I wanted to visit family and friends, so I decided to travel by driving alone — something I never thought I would do. I left my home in Ohio and headed 200 miles to Paintsville, Kentucky, where I had gone to high school. Another time, I drove ten hours to see my son in Raleigh, North Carolina, passing through Virginia and West Virginia on the way. It was fun just driving while listening to my favorite country music. I felt like I was becoming a "free spirit."

Now that I am 79, I realize I have done quite a few unexpected things, like going parasailing in Florida with a "special friend" (who was 83 at the time). He and I also traveled to Juneau, Alaska, to see my daughter. While we were there, we took a helicopter trip to the ice fields. It was fantastic to be able to walk around on the ice in the middle of June. It was like being in another world.

This past year, I have been singing and playing guitar on "open mic" night every Wednesday on the patio of a local bar and grill called Gatsby's. The first time I went there, it was to see my son and his friend play. While watching them perform, I thought to myself, "I can do that!" So with my son accompanying me, I sang an Eddy Arnold song, "Anytime." I got a big ovation — which I assumed was because of my age.

Even though I have played the guitar since I was eight, I never dreamed I would play in front of an audience, especially in my 70s. Maybe I have finally found my niche in life. At least I think I have become an inspiration to the young women who come up and tell me that they hope they are like me when they are my age. It makes me want to keep on doing it.

Recently, for my 79th birthday, I went zip-lining at the Hocking Hills Canopy Tours in Rockbridge, Ohio, with my daughter, my granddaughter, her boyfriend, and some other seniors from the senior center. It was such a great day, they said they want to make it an annual event, so I'm sure we'll be doing it again this summer or fall. There was even an article with a picture of us (wearing our Zip Chicks t-shirts) in our local news!

At this time of my life, I feel lucky to have done so many unforgettable things. I am blessed to have my two grandchildren, ages 6 and 15, who live close to me. They are so important to me, and I hope that they will always remember the fun they had with Grandma, the free spirit.

38

RVing: Living Your Travel Dreams

by Jaimie Hall Bruzenak

Jaimie Hall Bruzenak is an RVer, author, and speaker. After writing *Support Your RV Lifestyle! An Insider's Guide to Working on the Road*, she teamed up with the late Alice Zyetz to publish several other books and e-books, including *Retire to an RV: The Roadmap to Affordable Retirement*. She traveled part-time as a solo RVer, and she now is on the road part-time with her husband, George. A popular speaker at educational RV events and shows, she also writes and blogs about the RV lifestyle on *RV Lifestyle Experts* at rvlifestyleexperts.com.

Travel — a dream often postponed — calls many of us. Travel takes you out of your normal life and circumstances. You see things from a different perspective. There's a risk that things could go wrong, and you may even perceive some danger. Whether these concerns are real or imagined, confronting new challenges is exhilarating and can lead to growth, even in your 70s. And what better way to travel than in your own RV "house"? What better time than now?

You can join the more than 30 million RV enthusiasts of all ages. And it doesn't have to cost an arm and a leg to get started. A used RV in good condition will do. RVs can be retrofitted for people with disabilities by adding ramps, lifts, or other aids. A smaller mobile space means less cleaning to do and no yard work!

Travel does not have to be that expensive either. Camping fees and fuel costs can by kept down by the choices you make. Boondocking (dry camping with no hookups) is free on many of our public lands. By using solar panels and an inverter, you can stay several days without having to take on water or dump your wastes. Camping clubs offer half-price rates and other discounts for securing lower-cost RV sites. You could travel for shorter distances, stay longer, and save on fuel. Some RVers work or volunteer as they travel, often scoring a free RV site in the process. They have the added satisfaction of giving back or earning income, bringing structure to their lives, and exploring beautiful places.

Where can you go? Wherever you want! National parks, historic sites, forests, deserts, and the ocean are all there for you — pick new scenery whenever you want a change. RVs are also ideal for visiting family and friends. You bring your own bed, bathroom, and food. Park in a driveway, or a few miles down the road in a campground, for just the right balance of closeness and privacy.

You can pursue hobbies and interests as you travel, too. My friend Chuck traveled in his RV to bridge tournaments well into his 80s, finding teammates among others who did not have a regular partner. He also met square-dance partners and musicians to jam with in his travels.

What if you are alone? A number of RVers travel solo. It may surprise you to learn that more women than men travel by themselves in an RV. RVing Women is a club that teaches classes on operating your RV. There are also solo groups in other RV clubs, both in the United States and internationally, that offer companionship and support.

One woman, Shirley, retired from a second career at 72 and took up RVing. For her, it's about the adventure; she feels it keeps her from stagnating and getting "old." She travels to beautiful places, often painting what she sees.

RVing is a way to stay active both mentally and physically, keeping you fit, engaged, and young. An RV can be the vehicle to make your travel dreams come true.

39

Taking Charge of Your Health at 70

by Ruth Heidrich, Ph.D.

Ruth Heidrich, Ph.D., although retired, is an author, speaker, nutritionist, talk-show host, and triathlete. Living in Honolulu, Hawaii, she trains in running, biking, and swimming all year round. Still competing, she's won over 900 medals and was named one of the "Ten Fittest Women in North America" by *Living Fit Magazine*. Her books include *A Race for Life*, which details her struggle to beat her fast-metastasizing cancer; *The Race for Life Cookbook Chef*; and *Senior Fitness*. Her Web site is at ruthheidrich.com.

So, you're looking at your 70s? Your youth is long gone — heck, even middle age is just a distant memory! You know you're getting "up there" when you look at 60-year-olds as "youngsters." Then you realize that your 60s weren't so bad after all — actually, they were pretty good! But, hey, you're not "old" — "old" is anyone ten years older than you!

Looking ahead, you realize you're facing health challenges you never dreamed could happen to you. Whether you're worried about your heart, blood pressure, joints, or bladder — you've decided to start taking better care of yourself. You may need to begin a healthy diet and exercise program. Studies suggest that many afflictions, including heart disease, most cancers, strokes, diabetes, hypertension, osteoporosis, arthritis, ED, and dementia can be prevented or reversed. Don't wait for a health crisis to occur. If you're really smart, you'll be proactive and do a little preventive maintenance — to keep what you've got or regain what you might have lost.

If you're still with me, I can save you a ton of time in researching the best diet and exercise program, one that will take you through the next 30 years, plus or minus a few. Studies have shown that the people who live the longest, those who are active and healthy at 100, follow a mostly plant-based diet of whole foods and are still engaged in work of some kind.

The Live-to-100 Diet

The best foods are whole-plant foods, selected from a variety of fruits, vegetables, and whole grains — all natural and full of complex carbohydrates, adequate amounts of protein and fat, and loaded with antioxidants that neutralize free radicals, which age our body and brain. Since no nutrient acts alone, it is best to get whole foods, which are rich in nutrients. No refining, no processing, no adding or subtracting anything.

The Live-to-100 Exercise Program

Every system in the body follows Wolff's Law, which, in essence, states: use it or lose it. If muscles and bones don't get stressed, they atrophy. Aerobic-type exercises are best for pushing oxygen and nutrients to the brain, and to help in forming new neural connections. The best exercise program is the one that you make a habit of doing!

The 10-Day Program

For the next ten days, follow a diet of whole fruits, veggies, and whole grains. Here's my recommendation for a sample meal plan: try a breakfast of oatmeal and blueberries; for lunch, have a large spinach/tomato/carrot salad; for dinner, make a brown-rice pilaf with five or six different veggies. To develop an exercise regimen, schedule the first hour of your day for a run, a walk, a swim, biking, or weight lifting.

And if you like the results, schedule the next 30 years for more of the same!

Resources

Prevent and Reverse Heart Disease
by Caldwell B. Esselstyn, Jr., M.D.

Dr. Neal Barnard's Program for Reversing Diabetes
by Neal D. Barnard, M.D.

Power Foods for the Brain
by Neal D. Barnard, M.D.

The McDougall Program: 12 Days to Dynamic Health
by John A. McDougall, M.D.

Healthy at 100
by John Robbins

40

Just Move It

by June Lands

June Lands, who lives in Ponte Vedra Beach, Florida, is grateful for having been born and reared in northeastern Alabama — a land blessed with spirited people and outrageous tellers of tales. But now, at age 81, she's a toasty-tan Florida girl. Lands is a columnist for the *Ponte Vedra Recorder*, and her work has also appeared in the *Christian Science Monitor*, the *Florida Times-Union*, and other publications. She enjoys walking the beaches and bringing home shells and rocks. She befriends kids and dogs and fishermen. And she writes about them all.

Hard-rockin' music pulled me from my car early one "almost spring" morning. I had come for the annual 5K Run/Walk taking place on the sand of our local beach, alongside the Atlantic Ocean.

I was there to celebrate life. I'd never done a Run/Walk before. I would be walking, not running. I was not a runner. A mature walker was what I was.

The runners were easily spotted — they wore "outfits."

Most were stretching. The rest of us, the walkers, were in whatever we had pulled out of the closet at 6:00 a.m. — or had awoken in. I watched, all the while wondering if I should try to stretch. No, I'd probably fall — or even worse, freeze in a stretch and not be able to move.

Also, I noticed that everyone else had a number pinned to their shirtfront. I had a paper with a number on it but no way to attach it to myself. Maybe they had done these events before and knew to bring safety pins. Should I just not worry about it? Actually, the number had to be visible, not wadded up and stuck in your shorts pocket (where mine was at the moment). Finally I walked to the check-in and got pins.

Trying not to call more attention to my rookie self, I wandered down to the beach to check out the sand like I knew what I was doing. I pronounced it packed and perfect.

About the time I decided I was out of my mind to do this foolish thing and should have stayed in bed till at least seven and grabbed the morning paper and gone to Starbucks for a café mocha, the sun broke from behind a cloud and bounced off the faces of a bunch of intense, energetic people. Forget "mature." In that moment, I was one of those intense, energetic people. And when the starter yelled, "GO," I did.

Since I didn't die on the way to the finish line and actually completed the race, I was pumped — a new term I learned that day. I even stopped at the grocery store for some unnecessary items, so I could walk up and down the aisles with my running shoes on and my number still pinned to the front of my shirt.

That 5K (3.1 miles) Walk awakened something in me. So much so that when I told my daughter, Missy, about my newfound fun, she mentioned that the annual Peachtree Road Race in Atlanta was coming up July 4. It would be special to do that together; she'd run, and I could walk or run-walk the 10K (6.2 miles). I said, "Sign me up." We did that race together for three different years.

Though I no longer participate in run/walks, I continue to walk for enjoyment and exercise, as well as to share "walker friendships." Nearly anyone can do it: just put one foot in front of the other, over and over and over again.

Hey, I think you've got it!

41

Saving the World

by Kat Tansey

Kat Tansey left corporate consulting to become an award-winning author, educator, and radio-show host. She is the founder of Choosing to Be Fit, a multimedia, educational approach to health and fitness for women in midlife and beyond. Tansey lives in Ojai, California, with her partner, Greg, and her Maine Coon cat, Mombasa, both of whom are part of the CTBF team. Learn more about what they are up to at choosingtobefit.com or facebook.com/ChoosingToBeFit. Excerpts from Tansey's first book, *Choosing to Be*, can be found at choosingtobe.com.

I nearly succeeded in killing myself 30 years ago, so, in a sense, I've lived two lifetimes. I hadn't thought of it that way until I sat down to write this piece.

I was 40 years old, and although I didn't believe it then, I was one of the lucky ones. The barrier of propriety and secrecy that had prevented me from getting the help I needed was smashed to pieces when paramedics broke down the door to save my life. I spent two days in critical care, after which, as required by California law, I was held in the hospital for 72 hours. This gave the psychiatrist an opportunity to convince me to spend two more weeks there, during which time I was given a book by Lenore Walker entitled *The Battered Woman*. The curtain of suppression and denial was lifted.

I was no longer silent. I volunteered on a rape and battering helpline. I took a kick-ass self-defense course. Our coach was Geena Davis, who was making the groundbreaking movie *Thelma and Louise*. At our graduation, each of us battled a fearsome padded man while our family and friends cheered us on, and later gave us flowers when we received our diplomas.

In 1992, to help me heal from depression caused by the end of my career and life as I knew it, I began writing *Choosing to Be*. Little was known about Chronic Fatigue Syndrome back then, so I had to figure out how to get well. I did that in 5 years, but it took almost 20 years to finish the book and get it published. It has since become a well-loved inspirational book that has helped people worldwide, and I continue to receive notes from people telling me how it saved their lives. Despite these accomplishments, the past few years have included chronic stress, financial upheaval, and a string of personal injuries and setbacks. When I tried to stand up after squatting to plant herbs in my garden and didn't have the stamina or balance to do so, I knew it was time to take on another battle.

As part of my plan to regain my fitness and vitality, I've been writing *Choosing to Be Fit*. But this time it will be more than a book — it will be more like a movement. Women learned to take responsibility for their own safety many years ago. Now we need to access the wealth of information available and make the necessary connections to take responsibility for our own health and fitness.

In a conference in Vancouver in 2009, the Dalai Lama said, "The world will be saved by the Western woman." I am connected on LinkedIn, Facebook, and Google Plus with amazing women all over the world who are changing the face of health care, fitness, and aging. They are the hope for our future, and I am grateful to still be here, to be able to do what I can to help save the world.

42

Earthwatch Adventures After Age 70

by Warren Stortroen

In 1996, two months after retiring from the Principal Financial Group of Des Moines, Iowa, Warren Stortroen was watching birds from a blind in Costa Rica's cloud forest. This was Stortroen's first Earthwatch expedition, and he was hooked. He has now participated in 75 of them, and he's already signed up for three more. He lives in St. Paul, and when he's home, he volunteers with the Minnesota Valley National Wildlife Refuge, Minnesota Department of Natural Resources Scientific and Natural Areas, and several related organizations.

There was splashing and commotion in the water ahead of our boat, and as we approached we saw that a bald eagle had a salmon too big to fly with, so it was swimming the fish to shore; we rounded a point and suddenly a brown bear on the beach whirled and disappeared into the willows; a mother black bear with two young cubs watched us from a gravel bank; then, we heard pitiful cries and saw a furry ball floating on the surface — a sea otter pup was waiting for his mother to return from a dive for food. This all happened on one of our daily boat trips on the Earthwatch research expedition Sea Otters of Alaska, in wild and scenic Prince William Sound!

I was with five other volunteers who were gathered at the seaplane base in Cordova and flown by Beaver floatplane into Alice Cove. There, we were housed in comfortable platform tents with a cozy log cabin for a meeting place, meals, and evening activities. The research involved observation and photo IDing the otters, shore mapping, and bottom sampling. The volunteers and staff were great to work with and the sea otters were wonderfully entertaining. It was my first Earthwatch expedition after turning age 70 and a great way to embark on this milestone age!

Shortly after that, I was in Phimai in northeast Thailand for the Earthwatch archeological expedition Origins of Angkor. The scenario was like a Victorian-era dig, in the little village of Ban Non Wat, with a main excavation that was 5 by 25 meters and 5 meters deep and a smaller, deeper pit that required us to use ladders to get in and climb out. About 42 villagers did the heavy digging, screening, and washing of artifacts, and the volunteers did excavation after burial sites and artifacts were found.

The research was at the Neolithic level, dating from 1600 BCE and earlier. Some graves that we excavated had shell ornaments on the skeletons, and most had three ceramic pots near the head.

When we were not digging, some volunteers helped reconstruct pottery and the rest of us helped a team of three village ladies sort the pottery shards for rims and unique patterns. We didn't speak the same language, but they were very jolly and fun to work with! My most exciting moment was when I was excavating a pile of large pottery shards and some bones and teeth fell out! We called in the bone specialists, and they determined it was a child burial in a pot.

These are just two of the many Earthwatch adventures I've been on. Fifty-two of those have been after I turned 70, and I've thoroughly enjoyed every one! Earthwatch Institute is a unique nonprofit organization offering expeditions for volunteers to work with prominent research scientists on projects all around the world. The Web site at earthwatch.org provides information on current expeditions. It is a great way to enrich your retirement years — before and after turning 70!

43

My Big-Rig Dream

by Margarette Kirsch with Mary Farrell

Margarette Kirsch, a vibrant 84 years young, lives her life with panache! Whether riding a moped, a motorcycle, or a Segway, she is always ready for adventure. At 82, Kirsch finally fulfilled her lifelong dream to ride across America in an 18-wheel tractor-trailer, thanks to the Twilight Wish Foundation. Kirsch grew up in Rome, Georgia, during the Great Depression, went to college for two years, then worked for Lockheed Aircraft and American Airlines. She has been happily married to her husband, Jack, for 55 years. They reside in Merritt Island, Florida.

Mary Farrell is the director of community relations for the Twilight Wish Foundation, the first national wish-granting organization for the elderly, which has granted more than 1,880 wishes to low-income seniors and nursing-home residents aged 68+.

Riding cross-country in a big rig at 82? You bet! I have always said that I don't want to get to the end of my life and find that I have lived just the length of it . . . I want to have lived the width of it as well!

My adventure started in 2007, when I read an article about the Twilight Wish Foundation, an organization that grants wishes to senior citizens. I was skeptical, but I called the number in the article anyway. Founder Cass Forkin answered the phone and asked me my wish. I told her I've always wanted to be a truck driver or a showgirl. Cass said she would be in touch!

I've always lived my life with gusto, and for four years, I went to bed every night saying "road trip or showgirl." Finally, the call came! Although the showgirl wish fell through, Cass said the 18-wheeler trip was doable, and I jumped on it. Cass and her crew flew down to my house so I could meet them and my truck driver, Annabella Wood. In her early 50s, Annabella is a retired truck driver with 30 years on the road — and she's a country singer. We hit it off famously!

After their visit, all the logistics were worked out. Twilight Wish raised the money for this wonderful, earth-shaking trip and mapped out the route, which would take Annabella and me through 17 states in 15 days!

Finally, in June 2011, I packed my clothes for the journey — and my boots with three-inch heels, because they make me feel and look good, and I would not be happy sitting in the truck, talking to people and not giving them 100 percent of my personality.

The Penske truck was waiting for us in Dublin, Pennsylvania, with a great send-off from supporters and the press. Everyone wanted to see this 82-year-old woman in three-inch-heeled boots get in the 18-wheeler and drive away. On the trip, I learned how to get in and out of the truck, get on the windshield and on the side of the truck, check the oil, and pump the gasoline. I felt like I could drive a truck after watching Annabella change the gears and ease in and out of traffic and service stations so effortlessly, demonstrating precision driving and thinking. We talked continuously and never ran out of things to say.

We marveled at the gorgeous scenery as we drove, and we enjoyed stopping at several nursing facilities to meet the residents. We sat and talked with them for hours, at times singing and dancing. It was just a wonderful experience on the road from Pennsylvania to California and back to Merritt Island, Florida. Was I starstruck? A little bit! I had the time of my life! All this was done for me as a Twilight Wish recipient.

Thank you, thank you to Cass Forkin and the Twilight Wish Foundation!

To contact Twilight Wish, visit their Web site at twilightwish.org, or call (877) 893-9474.

44

The Place Where You Live

by Michael Milone, Ph.D.

Michael Milone, Ph.D., is a research psychologist based in New Mexico. At 68, he runs marathons whenever his knees let him and cross-trains with biking, swimming, skiing, and snowshoeing. On a more creative note, he managed to convince Arena Press to publish three of his novels, all of which are available online.

Memorable experiences don't have to be half a world away. If you explore the area where you live, you will undoubtedly make some remarkable natural, cultural, and social discoveries. Almost everyone can find something extraordinary within a day's drive of home.

A good way to start is to do a search of museums and other cultural centers, including the oddities. If you live near a major metropolitan area and have never been to one of the big museums like the Metropolitan Museum of Art (New York), the Field Museum (Chicago), or the Fine Arts Museums (San Francisco), you should definitely put them on your list. They are among the greatest museums on Earth, and your visit to any of them will never be forgotten. Do a little reading about the museums ahead of time so you are aware of the secret places in all of them and any special exhibits they are featuring.

But the "bigs" aren't the only museums worth visiting. The offbeat places can be just as entertaining and informative. The Mütter Museum of the College of Physicians of Philadelphia is devoted to medical history, but its collection is far more exciting than its name implies. I won't tell you too much about this unexpected treasure, but on your visit you might help to solve the mystery of the Soap Lady.

Get your exercise by checking out some new places to take a walk, a hike, or a bike ride. My wife and I have the good fortune to live in New Mexico, so the options available to us are endless, ranging from climbing Wheeler Peak (New Mexico's highest point at 13,167 feet) to following a newly discovered trail in the public lands near our home.

Admittedly, we are spoiled because of our location,

but there is no place in America that doesn't have distinctive places to walk, hike, or bike within a comfortable drive. When I travel for business, I always try to find an interesting place to run, and I've never been disappointed. Municipal or regional Web sites are a great resource and typically link to a map that makes it easy to find a route.

If you are driving to a museum or hiking spot, make the trip even more worthwhile by checking out the *Roadside Geology* series and getting a copy of the book for your area. These books are easy to read yet are full of fascinating information. Either preview your route ahead of time or bring a companion with you to read about the terrain through which you are passing. I don't want to be blamed for your having a driving incident while reading!

Some of my friends have promised themselves that they will visit every state or national park, recreation area, and other similar destination in their state. That's an admirable goal, and one that will certainly be fulfilling. If you suggest this to your significant other or friends, however, be prepared for doubting eye rolls. Despite their skepticism, it would be quite an adventure wherever you live.

45

Seventy

by Michele Hanson

Michele Hanson taught music in inner-city schools for 25 years and began writing humorous columns on local government for *The Guardian* in 1985. She gave up teaching in the mid-'90s and became a full-time freelance journalist and writer, commenting mainly on family life. Her books *Treasure* and *What Treasure Did Next* were made into a BBC animated cartoon, and *Living with Mother* won the 2007 Mind Book of the Year Award. Hanson's most recent books are an autobiography, *What the Grown-ups Were Doing*, and *Absolutely Barking: Adventures in Dog Ownership*. She lives in north London with her Boxer dog.

I n two days I'll be 70 whole years old. I don't quite know how to regard this: grim, I'm one year closer to the grave; or miraculous, I'm still here, even if I am creeping about in my elastic knee bandage. I had to put it on for my dog walkie last week. That's the trouble with being 70. The body can be such a letdown. You'd like to run about, climb trees, dig the garden, have a dance, and skip up and down stairs, but it hurts.

My friend Fielding loves running, poor chap. He used to run four miles, four times a week. Not anymore. Last month he felt really good. "I'm going to run UP a hill," he decided. And he did. A bit. Then *ping*! went his hamstring. No wonder some older persons are drinking more than the permitted amount, which seems rather measly anyway. I drank four times more on Saturday, but I was at my pre-birthday dinner party with chums and we all rather overdid it, which helped us to forget our impairments: irregular heartbeats, poorly knees, high blood pressure, Sjogren's syndrome, indigestion, arthritis, un-bendy back, tinnitus, trigger-finger, and mild Murray Valley fever virus — and I discovered yesterday that my neighbor Rosemary, 74, is deaf as a post.

I rang her doorbell and telephone and battered at her door until the neighbors rose up in protest. Was she dead inside? No. I know because I found her hidden keys — any fool could — broke in, and there she was, tottering about the silent garden, longing for one of those lift-yourself-up kneelers with handles.

But I don't want to throw you all into a glump about

the future. We all vary. Toad, the party host, 63, can still stand on his head, and Olga, 69, after a lifetime of yoga, cycling, and pottery, can do anything. Only last week she tore off my garage roof and ripped out Daughter's fitted wardrobe, more or less bare-handed. And our cooking is divine, our jokes brilliant; we've been friends forever and still are. So I think it's cup half full. Hanging on, and still having fun, fun, fun.

This essay was originally published in *The Guardian* (U.K.) and is reprinted with permission.

46

Beauty and Wisdom, at 70

by Robbie Kaye

Originally from New York, Robbie Kaye resides in Southern California and studied photography at the University of Southern California. Her work from her photography exhibit *Beauty and Wisdom* has been featured at Guate Photo 2012, Guatemala; in *D: la Repubblica*, Rome, Italy; at Camerawork Gallery, Portland, Oregon; Jeanie Madsen Gallery, Santa Monica; Perfect Exposure Gallery, Los Angeles; the Center for Fine Art Photography, Fort Collins, Colorado; Month of Photography, Los Angeles Group Show, Smashbox Studios; in *LensCulture*; *Lenscratch*; and F-Stop, *A Photography Magazine* (online). A recipient of International Aperture Awards, Kaye has permanent exhibits at USC and coauthored *Rendezvous with Light* with Carol Muske Dukes, California Poet Laureate.

My photography exhibit *Beauty and Wisdom* unfolded from the idea of a photographic series documenting an entire day at a specific place (a junkyard, an antique mall, etc.). I thought that a salon session would be a whimsical scenario: I could photograph a narrative portrait series of women getting their hair washed, sitting in curlers, and having their nails done. However, my outlook changed the day I arrived at the beauty parlor. I saw the women through the lens of my camera, isolated in frame, and I discovered their strength, beauty, and integrity. The first session was with Jenny, 71 years old. Under the modern dryer, which covered part of her eyes and her curlers, she struck a pose without any prompting from me, and I could not help but notice her elegance. From that moment, I knew that this project would be much more than a fun day at the beauty parlor. It became my goal to alter the public's perception of beauty and aging, and to create visibility for this otherwise overlooked generation.

As I approached my 50th birthday, the women I interviewed for *Beauty and Wisdom* gave me courage. When I listened to each of their stories, I feared aging less. Whether it was Rose Hall, 71, who swims every morning; Yoshi, 78, who plays golf every week; or Eunice, 75, a hairstylist who works every single day because she loves her job, it didn't take much for me to see that their age did not matter at all. What did matter was the connection they felt to life, to other people, and to themselves. Physically active or not, they were vibrant and emergent.

My own grandmothers were ageless role models. One of them, the matriarch of Queens, New York, traveled while in her 70s, managing to balance the care of her husband, herself, and her family. She kept up with fashion, current events, and life. She did not slow down in her 70s. Instead, she made room for the things she enjoyed, especially shopping. Always dressed impeccably, she never complained about age. I believe that the universe responds to the things we say and feel. Perhaps that is why she lived into her 90s.

These beautiful and wise women don't identify with societal preconceptions about aging. They thrive, despite a culture that focuses heavily on the beauty of youth. Smart, sexy, and distinguished, they are to be revered and honored as an integral part of our society, even as they pave the way for the rest of us. In my opinion, these women should be on billboards everywhere — then everyone would see that beauty is ageless, and that age is beautiful in every way. Joni Mitchell, who happens to be turning 70 this year, once sang about learning that no woman is an "old woman." And I learned that too.

47

Athletics for Aging Well

by Rose Marie Ray

Rose Marie Ray, the author of *SuperWomen Do IT Less . . .* and *From Broken Neck to Broken Records*, was an information technology sales executive and a pathbreaker for women in computing. As the "Speaker in Residence" for Texas Woman's University, she supported women in transition in the workforce. She has been an inn owner/innkeeper and is currently a hospitality-industry management consultant. Competing on the state and national levels in cycling and triathlon for the past six years, Ray holds Georgia and Florida state records in time trials and was a silver medalist in triathlon at the 2011 Senior Olympics.

My partner, Sandy, and I are in great company as we journey through our 70s. He and I believe that we are aging well, with just some wrinkles and gray hair. As athletes, we are getting out every day — riding bicycles, swimming, running, walking, golfing, or playing tennis — and moving at more than turtle speed. Sometimes, we are doing three things in a day and enjoying the camaraderie of friends. Vacations are with pals who share the joy of travel: skiing down a mountain together for a week, ending the day with a group meal, meeting at cycling races and triathlons on a local, state, and national level, and always having fun.

Florida living gives us the distinct advantage of fine weather, which is welcoming to those who love being outdoors. Taking an open-water swim on a Friday morning with friends and sharing breakfast on a porch with a water view is an ideal way to end the week — or to begin the weekend, for those who are not retired.

Many of my close friends have been athletes for their whole lives, participating in endurance sports like cycling, triathlon, marathons, and short road races. Sports are just as important to them now as when they were young. The pace is slower, but the desire to achieve their best effort and to win is still alive and well. The common thread as 70-year-olds is sharing the experience of good health and strong bodies and minds.

Just what is it that makes older athletes special? Some of the women who have worked and raised their children are now enjoying free time to do what they love. Other older athletes seem to thrive on the determination and discipline that are required for success. Maybe a pacemaker or other medical concern is a constant reminder that they need to be active. Perhaps a desire for recognition drives them to continue to compete.

Whatever our personal motivation, companionship is something that we all share. Those of us who are athletic in our 70s and 80s belong to a group where members are concerned for each other. We work out together at least four or five times per week, and we keep in touch always. Some of us like to ride our bikes many miles per day together and then hit a few races. Others like to take a short run and swim and then ride for a moderate distance and do many races. It's been wonderful to see that survivors of heart attacks and cancer in our group of friends do not give up and become couch potatoes. With the support of family and friends, they — and all of us — excel at living well as master athletes.

48

When 70 Isn't 60

by Ilene Little

Ilene Little is the CEO of Traveling 4 Health & Retirement (THR). She started this consumer-reporting Web site to facilitate unfiltered conversations between consumers and international medical and lifestyle professionals, as well as people who travel overseas for treatment or to manage their health-care needs. Little has the exclusive medical-tourism blog on *EscapeArtist.com*. In addition, she hosts the *Know Before You Go* show, broadcast weekly at overseasradio .com. She's also on the Web sites of several physicians and medical researchers, and is quoted in *Saving Private Healthcare* by Michael Kalthoff. Her own book is *How to Plan a Successful Medical Tourism Trip*.

As baby boomers pass through life, they change everything in their path, and that includes the myth of what life is like in one's 70s. Statistics reveal that people live longer and stay more youthful at age 70 than seniors had been in previous generations.

The elderly people you might typically see today

in senior centers and retirement homes across the U.S. represent those previous generations and are not necessarily representative of aging boomers. For example, I know many people in their 70s who are insulted by how seniors are portrayed as silly, dithering stereotypes on TV sitcoms — it's demeaning.

I loved the movie *The Best Exotic Marigold Hotel* for its portrayal of scenarios where high-spirited seniors resist the efforts of "well-meaning" relatives to organize their lives. That movie has a lot to teach adult children about people in their 70s. The way I see it, today's age 70 is the age of the "roaring 70s" and the bucket list and breaking free from all but self-imposed restraints.

Energy-wise you can feel younger at 70 than you did at 60 because chances are you've been retired long enough to get past the speed bumps of retirement planning. You've faced those limitations and are now ready to move on.

Late Bloomings and New Beginnings

Approaching the big 7-0, there's a shift in mindset. We're thinking about punching through our bucket list while we're still healthy.

The very act of implementing that list has surprising health benefits. Each new experience breathes new life and energy into old bones. Forget the old saying "you can't teach an old dog new tricks." Indeed, you can! By taking a few precautions to give your body a break — like better shoes and the luxury of a daytime nap — you can accomplish anything your imagination can envision.

The bucket list becomes the catalyst for a positive change in consciousness. Everyone I've interviewed says the experience of checking off the "must dos" on their list leaves them feeling decades younger and stronger mentally. After completing the sojourns and activities they've long dreamed about, they use words like "at peace" and "mental space" to describe the afterglow they feel. This time in our lives can be as exciting and meaningful as we want it to be!

49

Still Sailing After All These Years

by Ed Howle

Ed Howle and his wife, Janet, are well over 65, and they currently consider themselves novelists. Both of them have had several other careers, none of which contributed to their decision to write fiction. It has been their life experiences that provide material for their writing. Their debut novel, *The Long Road to Paris*, is based on their around-the-world antique-car rally, travels in Asia, and years of living in Paris. In addition, they are avid ocean sailors. Their new novel-in-progress is set on a sailboat in the Bahamas. At this point in their lives, they divide their time between their home in North Carolina, sailing, and international travel.

T hree years ago I fell, split open my forehead, and broke two ribs. The physician's assistant who first saw me said that a person of my age needed to have "a personal relationship with a doctor." That's okay with me as soon as I find one who will follow me, now 78, through the Bahamas. Boredom for me is deadly, and I intend to do what I want as long as I am able. Fortunately, my wife, Jan, is equally adventurous, and we have modified our sailing to make it "age appropriate."

Many aging sailors move to power boats, but it didn't work for us, so this year we bought a new 39-foot sailboat and outfitted it to keep sailing. This boat is small enough for the two of us to manage yet large enough for comfortable onboard living. It has a center-line berth so either of us can get up in the night without disturbing the other. We've kept our dingy, outboard motor, and anchor lightweight, added an electric winch, to make sail-handling easier, and a bow-thruster to assist in docking. We are also equipped with a marine GPS, which will help us with navigation.

We took delivery of the boat on the Gulf Coast of Florida, and the first week was a challenge; we had to deal with a new boat with fancy electronics *and* a new sailing territory. We never have liked long passages, but to get through the Florida Keys to Miami, we faced two stretches that required an overnight sail. We were grateful when, on the first leg of our trip, the wind died, allowing us to just drop anchor and get a good night's sleep. What we didn't know was that we had tangled a crab-pot line; the next morning I had to dive under the boat to free the propeller. It's been a long time since I've had to test myself this way, but what option did I have? Jan wasn't diving. In the end, with tangled line in hand, I had a real sense of accomplishment.

With no other mishaps, other than an exhausting overnight leg from Marathon in the Florida Keys, we arrived safely in Miami. The Gulf Stream has a well-deserved reputation for nasty seas. We waited for a forecast of waves less than four feet and light winds. That day came and we set out, but the forecast was wrong and we had strong winds and waves over the bow. We stayed in the cockpit, reducing the risk of seasickness, and reminded ourselves that even this motion was preferable to a porch rocking chair.

The key to sailing is both physical and mental flexibility. This seems a good formula for conquering aging too. We have been tested by unexpected weather, rough seas, long passages, and repairs, but we feel younger and more capable than when we started.

The weather at home in North Carolina is sleet and ice, but for at least one more year, we'll set sail for a warmer climate. The sunny Exumas are waiting!

50

A Time to Dance!

by Karen O'Connor

Karen O'Connor is an award-winning author of more than 70 books, including the best-selling series from Harvest House *Gettin' Old Ain't for Wimps* and *Help, Lord! I'm Having a Senior Moment* from Regal Books. A popular speaker, O'Connor is also a writing mentor for the Mount Hermon Christian Writers Conference and the Jerry B. Jenkins Christian Writers Guild. To find out more, visit O'Connor's Web site at karenoconnor.com.

Dance is the hidden language of the soul.

— Martha Graham

When I turned 70, I was determined to do one thing that year — dance! One night, as my husband, Charles, and I watched a televised musical tribute to the great Ella Fitzgerald, I suddenly felt young and carefree again.

"How High the Moon," "Dream a Little Dream of Me," and "The Man I Love," sung by such notables as Nancy

Wilson and Natalie Cole, took me back to my high school and college years of the 1950s, when I was a devoted fan of jazz.

Right then, I wanted to hold the man I love, dream a little dream with him, and gaze out the window at the moon high above. But I hardly seemed prepared for such romantic activities. There I sat, dressed in my old sweats, with no makeup, hair askew, and eyes squinting through glasses that needed a good cleaning. I'd restored my house that day after weekend guests had gone — but I hadn't pulled myself together yet.

Meanwhile, Charles was in the kitchen putting away food and dishes from dinner, scrubbing pots and pans, and commenting on the music and the memories it evoked. "That was a great era. They don't write love songs like those anymore," he said.

Suddenly I knew it was time — time to dance.

I peered over to Charles and smiled. "Dance with me?"

"Now?"

"Mmm." I held out my arms and swayed to the music.

"But I'm in the middle of —"

"I'm in the middle of something, too — of a longing — to dance."

"Okay." He walked around the half wall that divided the kitchen from the living room and took me in his arms, a sopping dish towel over one shoulder and an apron around his waist.

I put my left arm on his shoulder — the one without the wet towel — and fit my right hand into his left one. He pulled me close, sweatshirt to sweatshirt, and danced me all over our new hardwood floor, just made for dancing. The faux flames in the faux fireplace licked the faux logs as we whirled and twirled in front of them, both in our Ugg boots.

In my mind, however, I was wearing silver-strap stilettos and a close-fitting black dress with pearls around my neck, and Charles was clad in a navy-blue suit with a white shirt and cuff links, black Ferragamo loafers, and a smashing red-and-blue-striped Robert Talbott silk tie.

"We won't forget this night," I teased. "When one of us is gone, the other will remember the time when we danced the night away just the way we were, and didn't care a hoot about it — as long as we were holding each other close."

He nodded in agreement and smiled behind eyes wet with tears. I realized that for Charles, too, it was a time for dancing. He just hadn't realized it until I held out my arms. And so we danced and danced — the year I turned 70.

Excerpted from *The Upside of Downsizing: 50 Ways to Create a Cozy Life* (2011) by Karen O'Connor (permission from Harvest House Publishers).

51

The Fine Art of Napping

by Elaine M. Decker

Elaine M. Decker is a social satirist and recovering type A personality. After graduating from Brown University, Decker, a New Jersey native, worked in New York City. Following an early career in computers, she climbed a Fortune 500 ladder into consumer marketing, then dabbled in communications. She relocated to Providence, Rhode Island, in 1992. Continuing on her debatably logical career path, she migrated into nonprofit management, then retired to write and to refine her napping techniques. Her writing has been featured on BlogHer and in a column in *PrimeTime Magazine*, aimed at older adults in Rhode Island. She is the author of two books, *Retirement Sparks* and *Retirement Sparks Again*. Read her blog at retirementsparks .blogspot.com and her tweets @womaniacs.

One of the great joys of turning 70 is being able to take a nap whenever you want. After an in-depth study of the subject, I've identified many variations on the nap. Here are six of them.

1. The most familiar is the opportunistic catnap, so named because cats have perfected this midday

snooze. You can catnap anywhere, but the best place is stretched out on your back, usually on a couch, with the sun on your face. Not sure if the nap you're taking is this type? Check your midsection when you wake up. If there's a cat on top of you, you've just enjoyed a catnap.

2. Another type you'll recognize is the post-prandial nap, which occurs after a big meal. Septuagenarians become increasingly prone to these after having a sizable lunch. Careful observation of my family reveals that men are extremely fond of post-prandials, except when there's football on TV. These naps are most appropriately taken in an overstuffed chair. They're often short, yet highly effective. Just ask my cousin Louie.

3. The alcohol-induced nap is related to the post-prandial, but you don't need to have eaten before one. These are particularly welcome after wine tastings, especially the ones you have alone in your own home. Their duration depends on how much alcohol you've imbibed and whether you've collapsed onto something comfortable. Many of my most refreshing naps have occurred during what

some might call a "wine stupor." I prefer to think of them as research projects.

4. Those in their 70s will be familiar with the reading-induced nap. This is characterized by the body positioned in a cushy chair, reading material in hand. You may not realize you've had this nap until you wake up and find your eyeglasses on your lap and your book (or magazine or newspaper) on the floor. The older we get, the fewer pages it takes to induce a reading nap.

5. The older we get, the more we need exercise-recovery naps, which are most effective when you're splayed out on a pile carpet. When I mow our lawn, I have to lift the clippings catcher to shoulder height to empty it into those enormous brown paper sacks. This exhausts me more than the mowing itself. After I've finished, you'll find me nose-deep in the carpet, in a classic recovery snooze.

6. Lastly (of course) we have the procrastinator nap, best taken when you have a long list of projects that need attention, but you don't want to tackle any of them. This is another guilty pleasure for those turning 70. We can procrastinate as much as we

want without serious repercussions. Except, as I've learned, if the task at hand is writing one's weekly blog post.

As long as I've had my quota of catnaps and post-prandials, I can resist the procrastinator. I'm more likely to miss a posting because I've succumbed to an alcohol-induced nap. Speaking of which, now that this is done, I'm going to pour myself a nice glass of vino, sit back, and . . . zzzzzzz.

Part

3

NURTURING
YOUR SOUL

52

Seven (as in 70) Is a Spiritual Number

by Gary Zukav

Gary Zukav is the winner of the American Book Award, author of four consecutive *New York Times* best-sellers, including the legendary #1 *New York Times* best-seller *The Seat of the Soul*, and cofounder of the Seat of the Soul Institute. His insights, gentle presence, and 35 appearances on *The Oprah Winfrey Show* have endeared him to millions of viewers. Six million copies of his books are in print, and translations have been published in 32 languages. To contact Gary Zukav or learn about authentic power and spiritual partnership, visit www.seatofthesoul.com.

I f your life is not already focused on spirituality, this would be a good time to begin. *Spiritual* means pertaining to your soul. Your soul is that part of you that longs for harmony, cooperation, sharing, and reverence for Life. When you make these intentions your intentions, no matter what you are experiencing inside you or what is happening outside you, you create authentic power. Authentic power is the alignment of your personality with your soul.

By now, you have experienced the consequences of aligning yourself with the needs of parts of your personality that originate in fear, and that manifest as anger, vindictiveness, jealousy, or feeling superior and entitled, or inferior and needing to please, or craving alcohol, shopping, smoking, or sex (thoughts of exploiting others do not automatically diminish with time), etc. The consequences of acting with the energy of fear are always painful and destructive. Aging does not change this. Only your choices to act with love instead of with fear will change the consequences that you create for yourself. The consequences of acting with the energy of love are always blissful and constructive.

Why use your choices to create a life of competition, hoarding, discord, exploitation, and pain when you can use them to create a life of cooperation, sharing, harmony, reverence, and bliss? Why disempower yourself with closed and unhealthy thoughts such as "I don't have enough energy," or "I'm too old," when you can experiment with open and healthy thoughts such as "What can I contribute to Life?" or "What would it feel like to create with an empowered heart without attachment to the outcome?"

I suggest that you experiment with this dynamic whenever you feel a current of fear is active in you: before acting or speaking, change your intention from one that's based on manipulation and control to one that's focused on harmony, cooperation, sharing, or reverence for Life. Act or speak with that intention — or at least with the intention to understand, develop patience, or be in integrity with what you say, what you do, and what the most healthy, grounded, and wholesome part of your personality wants to do.

In my experience, this is the most rewarding thing anyone can do on any day of any year, including the year that you celebrate the 70th anniversary of your entrance into the Earth school.

53

Giving Back

by Jerry Osteryoung

Jerry Osteryoung is a consultant to businesses, and he has directly assisted over 3,000 firms. He is the Jim Moran Professor of Entrepreneurship (emeritus) and a professor of finance (emeritus) at Florida State University. Osteryoung was the founding executive director of the Jim Moran Institute and served in that position from 1995 through 2008. His newest book, coauthored with Tim O'Brien, is *If You Have Employees, You Really Need This Book*.

Our birthdays are feathers in the broad wing of time.

— Jean Paul Richter

On February 25, I turned 70, which is a milestone I never thought I would reach. All of a sudden, one day I just woke up, and I was having my 70th birthday.

As I prepared to celebrate this big event, I spent a considerable amount of time thinking about my life and what I have accomplished. I am fortunate to have had the opportunity to do a great many things in my 70 years, as a father, a professor, an entrepreneur, a writer, a community volunteer, a leader, and a mentor.

In each of these roles, I have tried to make a lasting impact on those around me. In addition to my kids and grandson, who are my legacy, I have gained a real sense of value when I've helped others without expecting anything in return.

During the course of my job at the Jim Moran Institute, I assisted thousands of entrepreneurs, and the same can be said of the hours I spent doing volunteer work. In six years as a counselor at 211 Big Bend, Leon County's crisis hotline, I guided many people through very difficult situations. As chairman of the board of both Goodwill Industries of Big Bend and the Florida Commerce Credit Union, I received zero pay, but I've always gotten tremendous satisfaction from the help I was able to provide.

The old cliché that you get more when you give from the heart is so true. Sure, I have done well financially, as I understand the value of saving and investing wisely; however, it is not financial gain that has given me joy in my life. Rather, it is the belief that, by giving of myself without expecting anything in return, I have truly been able to help people. I have been so blessed and have received so much as a result.

Businessmen have gotten a bad rap lately for being solely interested in making money. Without question, there are some out there who are only concerned with this, but many realize that there is a greater good in helping their community become better.

Consider the entrepreneurs you know who are truly successful. One thing they all have in common is that they go out of their way to make sure they give back to the community both as individuals and as a company.

Making money is great and a worthy goal, but a higher goal is helping people in need. Whether you are still working or you have retired from your former career, consider how you can reach out and help others. The people you help could be current or past coworkers, friends, or strangers. Whatever form of altruism you choose, I promise that you will see the value when, down the road, you look back on what you have accomplished in your life.

You can do this!

54

The Journey Continues

by Sandy Warshaw, LCSW

Sandy Warshaw, LCSW, is a Jewish, feminist, lesbian breast-cancer survivor, mother of two, grandmother of three, lifelong social-justice activist on behalf of herself and others. She has served on many boards, marched many marches, and for almost 30 years has been an advocate for midlife and older women. Warshaw is cofounder of SHARE, a self-help program for women with breast and ovarian cancer. Her biography is included in *Feminists Who Changed America* 1963–1975. At 72, she became a bat mitzvah and was awarded a 4th-degree black belt in World Seido Karate. "Aging to perfection" is her mantra.

My life in the 1970s began with a breast-cancer diagnosis. The next decades were times of "harvesting" wisdom. My 70s have been a time of self-realization and self-actualization built on the foundation of the three decades before.

At 53, I discovered karate, a physical and spiritual art matching my strength and need for focus. At 60, I became a black belt, and at 72, I earned the coveted title of "sensei" — teacher — and the unofficial title "role model" for younger *karatekas*, who saw they could train into their later years — grandmotherhood had a different look.

At 60, I joined Congregation Beit Simchat Torah in New York, the largest LGBT synagogue in the world. I studied Torah at Ma'yan, the Jewish Women's Project. At 72, a month before I became a *sensei*, I became a bat mitzvah, a ceremony that, in my youth, was reserved exclusively for Jewish boys. I learned Hebrew! Chanted from the Torah! Delivered a *drash* (sermon) before family and friends.

At 78, I thought about the fact that my mother had died at 79, and I realized I still had important work to do. I was not afraid of dying — but I wanted to "find God."

I intensified my spiritual search. I joined a new synagogue; took a class in "spiritual autobiography"; and began to explore where I had been and where I was going. Four of us formed our own spiritual-autobiography workshop, meeting and writing monthly. I outlined a list of conversations that we needed to have in our aging Jewish community, and this became the basis for a series about spiritual aging called "Grow Old Along with Me: The Best Is Yet to Be."

As I encouraged others to embrace both the adventures and hardships of aging, I faced my own limitations — emphysema from 30 years of smoking and a back that reflected the scoliosis of birth and the shrinking of age, causing imbalance and timidity. As I admitted such limitations, and gave up karate and the hope of the 5th-degree black belt, I dealt with my resentment and developed a determination to continue an active life — asking for help when I needed it — and using a cane — signs of "age"? Of "disability?" Or just reality! I updated my will, my living will, and my health-care proxy. I called my children together to make sure they knew my present financial state and my thoughts about my life and the end of life. I asked them what "things" they wanted, and began a process of decluttering those things they didn't want. I didn't want them to have to be burdened with doing that.

My karate teacher, the Grand Master of World Seido Karate, teaches: *So sen koh kai* ("No matter where they start, all rivers flow into the sea"). No matter what path we take to become a better person, if we stay the path, we will reach that goal. My karate, my synagogue life, my continued activism are the paths I have taken. They have defined my personhood in my 70s, and they will lead me through my 80s.

55

A Time for Contemplation

by Juan O'Callahan

Juan O'Callahan is an 80-year-old fitness and health expert and marathon runner. As an AFAA-certified personal trainer and a member of the National Council on Strength and Fitness, he concentrates on improving the lives of others his age and older. O'Callahan is a former Marine Corps jet pilot, engineer, business consultant, and entrepreneur who founded two aerospace-industry consulting firms. He created the Wellness for Super-Seniors fitness programs and is the author of *Wellness for Super-Seniors*. He and his wife reside in Connecticut, near their six children and 13 grandchildren. For more information, please visit juanswellness.com.

At 80, I can now look back and see clearly what I should have done as I approached 70. Back then, I was in too much of a hurry — until seven years ago, when I met Frank Ladwig, who became my friend and mentor, and who brought me back to earth.

After Frank retired as an executive in a major corporation, he became an adjunct professor at the

Boston College graduate School of Management, teaching M.B.A. class sections in personal marketing. Frank's ultra-popular courses were besieged with students who "simply had to get into Professor Ladwig's section."

Frank condensed his course into a manual entitled *The Seven-Sided Model for Developing the Whole Person*. It featured a heptagon with seven "Key Words" around the sides: Physical, Mental, Social, Professional, Family, Financial, and Spiritual. Frank would explore these themes throughout the semester, preparing his students for "real life" and business careers, while reminding them not to abandon their personal lives in the process.

Why is a college student's guide to career preparation appropriate for 70-year-olds? Quite simply, this type of introspection is invaluable at any age. It can benefit my grandchildren as they prepare to graduate from high school and move on to college or another path. It's also helpful for my adult children, who are in their early 50s. At age 70, men and women today are entering a new phase of their lives, which can be exciting and vibrant — if they consider their "seven sides."

After reassessing my own overall wellness condition,

I decided to become more physically fit. I ran races and a few marathons. I studied and got certified as a personal fitness trainer. With Frank's encouragement, I founded wellness classes for people over 75 and self-published a book, *Wellness for Super-Seniors*. I also became the guardian of an elderly cousin who had little other support, took up my painting again, tried golf, and deeply pondered matters of faith. In my 70s, I did things that I should have done years earlier.

Matters of faith — the "Spiritual" Key Word — may be the most-discussed aspect of Frank's teachings. I have found it beneficial to ask myself the following questions, and perhaps you will, too: Who am I? Where did I come from? What is "truth"? Where am I going? If I'm going, how am I going to get there? When am I going to get there? What is "good"? What is the ultimate answer to "life"?

Of course, when contemplating any of the Key Words, you can create your own questions. The point, I believe, is to really think about the questions you pose, calmly find all of the potential answers, and see how you can incorporate these insights into your life.

At a recent college commencement, Lou Holtz said,

"You don't have to necessarily be 'successful' — you should try to be significant." And as Frank Ladwig (who died in 2012, at age 95) noted in his manual, quoting the words of Walter Lippmann, "Touch life at every point and make life richer, fuller, and more splendid."

56

The View from 70: Reflections on Aging

by Judith Rich, Ph.D.

As a writer, trainer, teacher, and coach, Dr. Judith Rich has been instrumental in bringing transformation and consciousness seminars to individuals and organizations throughout the world since 1976. Having passed the threshold of 70 herself, Dr. Rich brings a lifetime of experience, insight, and wisdom to her work with others who are reaching this life stage. While maintaining a small coaching practice, she continues to travel the world, working with those who seek a new direction for their lives. Dr. Rich is also a featured contributor on the Huffington Post, where this essay first appeared. Please contact Dr. Rich at judith@ judithrich.com.

I f 50 is the new 30, and 60 is the new 40, then is it too far-fetched to assume that 70 is the new 50? As I approached my 70th birthday, someone suggested I call it "the 40th anniversary of my 30th birthday." While it's tempting to consider skirting the reality of the number of years I've spent on the planet, something is calling me to face it head-on — no cute little euphemisms about "70 being the new 50," etc. I think it's time to call a spade a spade.

While today's 70-year-old is nothing like the 70-year-olds of our parents' generation, there is no mistaking the fact that, by any measure, turning 70 marks the beginning of a whole new territory in life, one we used to call "old age." But what is "old," exactly? And what does it mean to be 70 in a society that worships youth, where people strive to maintain it at all costs?

Getting older is precisely what we tell ourselves it is. If we buy into the cultural stereotype of aging, then it probably means we will march in lockstep straight to the rocking chair of life and stay there.

But it doesn't have to be this way. We can age gracefully, not fighting or denying the fact, and even take a little "time out" in that rocking chair. But that doesn't mean setting up camp there and falling asleep! The rocking chair is a well-deserved respite, but for it to fulfill its function it must be kept in motion. And so must we. Staying in motion means more than just remaining physically active, which is important. It also means remaining mentally active, and learning to appreciate this stage of life as a new adventure. There is still much to be discovered! This time of life offers up many new possibilities for learning and engaging in creative expression.

In addition, we will also be given plenty of opportunities to let go of what is no longer necessary for the journey ahead. This may feel like loss on some level, and depending upon how we frame it, loss can either be the source of suffering or it can be freeing.

Who are you? Someday, your answer to that question will begin to shift, and you will find yourself in a place of uncertainty. After a lifetime of defining yourself one way, you discover that this identity no longer fits. At 70, you have likely already reached the point where you're no longer your title or your job description. You might still be somebody's wife or husband, mother or father, but is that who you *really* are?

Turning 70 is an invitation to reinvent yourself, to spread your wings and take flight into the new lands that await your discovery. Your wings are ready. Trust yourself and leap! And watch out for those 60-year-olds trying to keep up!

57

Embrace the Biggest Secret of Life

by LaTron Brown

LaTron Brown has dedicated his life to giving back and empowering others. He is passionate about senior living and health care. Currently, he is the owner of Senior Lifestyle Concierge, a boutique lifestyle-management service, providing the highest level of personal attention to ensure that seniors' needs are truly met. He serves as the marketing director of the Cultural Arts for Excellence 5K Family Fun Run/Walk and the community engagement chair of Urban Professional League. A member of the Alpha Phi Omega service fraternity, Brown graduated from Virginia Tech with a B.S. in psychology and biological sciences and holds an M.B.A. from Averett University.

People say that age is just a number. It is an axiom that some people wish to be true, others apply only in the moment, and few fully believe. As you reflect on 69 years, do not be dismayed. Realize that reaching the bottom of a calendar page does not symbolize an end — a simple flip of the page is only a beginning. Today, you might be in perfect health. You might encounter injury or illness. You might lose a loved one. You might fall in love. Embrace the power of possiblility that reveals itself throughout our lives, giving us the sense that *this* is how our life is supposed to be.

I have been blessed to recognize that the secret of life is experiencing the powers of presence and connection. It is commanding a life full of abundance and gratitude for every experience — good and bad. A verse in Psalms tells me that, even when facing tribulations, "my cup overflows." It is not about wishful thinking, taking a carefree approach to life, or acting like you are 21 again. Don't revert to the expectations of youth. Instead, focus on optimal living now.

When you decide how to experience each moment, you are encountering the power of presence. There is tremendous value in introspection, in reflecting on how all things have worked together to shape you into the person you have become. There are those in perfect health who are tired, depressed, and defeated. There are those who have a disease, yet they radiate with peace, power, and innocence. When I was a small child, my grandmother faced her biggest life challenge with Alzheimer's disease. What she never forgot was to have a song in her heart. She would sit in her favorite chair, rocking me in her lap and singing verses from her favorite church hymns. Those same hymns, I would later learn, are what got her through some of her most arduous circumstances. I now understand that, even in those challenging moments, she found peace within herself.

The power of connection is elicited by social and intellectual engagement. When we love, forgive, and teach, we are at our best. Utilizing your wisdom to help others is essential. Believe it or not, we are all dependent upon you. Your words bring progress. Your presence brings comfort. You are here for a reason. There is someone who needs you. As you connect, the gratitude that others express to you shows that you helped them reach *their* place of optimal living. Celebrating what you have to offer is where your legacy begins.

Indeed, age is just a number. Focusing on optimal living is a personal endeavor. You have to identify your wellspring of abundance, happiness, and peace. Growth is a never-ending process. When you understand optimal living, you do not give in to society's perception of aging. You reinvent it, and you become a beacon of change that our society needs.

58

The Thank-You Prayer

by Lewis Richmond

Lewis Richmond is a Buddhist teacher, author, and blogger. He has written four books, including the national best-seller *Work as a Spiritual Practice* (1999) and *Aging as a Spiritual Practice* (2012). He is the founder of Vimala Sangha, a Buddhist meditation group based in Mill Valley, California, and leads workshops and retreats on spirituality and aging in a variety of venues on the West Coast. Richmond is also a regular contributor to the Huffington Post's "Religion" section. His Web site is at lewisrichmond.com.

I n my book *Aging as a Spiritual Practice*, each chapter ends with a "contemplative reflection." These reflections are meditations, prayers, and inquiries that readers can use to explore their inner resources for coming to terms with aging, as well as to deepen their own natural elder wisdom.

One of the most popular reflections is a simple exercise I call the Thank-You Prayer. I came to this practice spontaneously one evening while sitting quietly, contemplating an azure sunset from my living-room window. I began reflecting on the words "thank you" — on how often we say them, sometimes unthinkingly, and how deeply they are embedded in our hearts. Along with numbers, they are among the first words we learn as children, and these two words are associated with more experiences and memories, perhaps, than any others.

So now I ask you to sit or rest comfortably, close your eyes, clear the inner landscape of your mind's eye of all distractions, and speak aloud or say silently to yourself, "thank you." Then, in the manner of free association or a reverie, just watch what comes to mind. It might be an image, a name, a phrase, or something like a dream. Don't censor or adjust this response. If you like taking notes, write it down. It could be something profound or seemingly trivial. In a workshop I was leading, one woman said, with some embarrassment, that what came to mind was the ham sandwich she had just had for lunch. Another woman said, with some surprise, "My hands." A man, who had earlier spoken of being saddened by a recent divorce, said with a sudden smile, "The taste of cinnamon."

Whatever comes to you is your deeper self's reply to the stimulus of these two simple words of gratitude — thank you.

Now do it again. Say "thank you" silently or aloud, and watch what comes. Again, note the response without judgment. It could be the same as before or something entirely different.

One of the universal experiences of growing older is loss, and the older we get the more these losses pile up. Of course, we have losses throughout our lives, but aging's losses — like the death of a friend or the vanishing of youthful vigor — are more likely to be serious and permanent. When I teach about aging, I speak candidly about loss; invariably, heads in the audience will begin to nod. But I also teach that with loss can come gratitude and a new appreciation for what we still have. In the thick of aging's difficulties, this gratitude can be disguised, but I've discovered that the Thank-You Prayer can coax it out. Scientists who study aging also confirm that feeling gratitude makes us measurably happier.

Try it a few more times. Say "thank you," and see what comes. When you have said it enough, open your eyes and rest in the recognition that at any age, in any life situation, gratitude is life's constant companion and ready gift.

59

Finding Fulfillment When You're 70 and Retired

by Maurine Patten

Certified lifestyle-transition mentor Maurine Patten helps working professionals transform their idea of retirement into an amazing, freedom-based lifestyle so they can tap into their dreams and make informed decisions that lead to a fulfilling life. Patten has reinvented herself many times in life and presents unique insights into this life stage she calls "an adventure that offers an expanded capacity for living and loving each day." As an agent of change, her mission is to help professionals create the life they really want rather than take the one that just shows up.

Retirement as it used to be is no more. What we now have is a new stage in life that may last for 20 to 30 years. There has never been a time like this in history. While this stage has yet to be named, the word *retirement* will eventually be retired.

So, what do we have in its place?

I find this gift of time of tremendous value. As a clinical psychologist in my early 70s, my mission is to spread the word about what is possible and help others create a freedom-based retirement lifestyle that is meaningful and joy filled.

I learned to do this in my own life. After I closed my private practice and sold my building at age 65, I knew I wanted to continue working. I spent several of my final clinical years preparing for the upcoming transition by getting certified in retirement coaching and taking classes in positive psychology.

During that time, I learned that we can use our character strengths to create a sense of happiness. When I locked my building for the last time, I felt ready for my own personal transformation. I knew at that point that our brain requires two important ingredients to feel fulfilled: novelty and challenge. When we encounter something novel, it releases a neurotransmitter for feelings of bliss and well-being. When we are faced with a challenge, it discharges a hormone that, in small amounts, elevates mood, increases concentration, and improves memory.

In addition, researchers know that the five strengths most closely related to life satisfaction are:

1. Gratitude — awareness and thankfulness for good things.
2. Optimism — realistically looking for the best in things.
3. Zest or vitality — living life as an adventure.
4. Curiosity — exploring and being resilient.
5. Love — valuing close relationships.

I use all five of these strengths to find opportunities for novelty and to challenge myself, which enhances my work and my life.

Also, I add the emotion of joy, which comes from feelings of happiness and well-being. Joy gives us the opportunity to broaden our outlook and to build our best future because it expands our ideas about possible options. It transforms us by touching and opening our hearts.

Yes, this life stage has its challenges. However, it can also be vital and amazing. I find I can take great pleasure in life by choosing to focus on:

- Having positive emotions.
- Using my strengths to be more engaged.
- Creating meaning in my life by helping others discover purpose in their lives.

- Experiencing feelings of accomplishment and fun in areas I personally value.
- Enjoying close relationships with my spouse of 52 years, adult children, grandchildren, and friends.

In spite of what is going on in my life and around me, I believe I have a choice about how upbeat I feel. I look for small things that will delight me, like going kayaking or seeing a blue sky or the stars at night. I also believe it's important to share happiness with others, helping them feel joyful so they can lead a more fulfilling life.

60

Sharing My Family Legacy

by Maeona (Mae) Mendelson, Ph.D.

Maeona (Mae) Mendelson, Ph.D., has begun an encore career as director of the Intergenerational Center at Chaminade University in Honolulu after serving six years as a volunteer board member of AARP and two years as chair of the AARP Foundation. She enjoys traveling with her husband, family, and four grandchildren.

I have been thinking about the markers and rites of passage in turning 70. After all, we receive the AARP card at age 50 and Medicare at 65. The answer came to me after my whole family left my birthday celebration. We span the globe and see each other three or four times a year. Now is the time to pay forward family legacies.

My husband is archiving 2,500 family photos. He identifies people, places, and occasions by year and scans each photo — the earliest is from the 1890s in Japan. We laugh about the fact that my family has better photographers than his. Out of these photo-documented years, we have spent 47 of them together — a lot of memories.

Our conversations about the photos remind me of my childhood in Japan. I know it's time for me to take my grandchildren there. Over four different trips, my mother took her grandchildren to visit ancestral homes and relatives. She left them with an indelible impression of what she valued. She shared with them an understanding of what contributed to a large part of their DNA — *ki* (awareness), obligation, civility, respect, excellence, and cultivation of beauty.

My motivation is different from my mother's. I want them to experience some of what I loved about growing up in Japan. After World War II, we left the relocation camp in Arkansas and settled on the East Coast. When my widowed mother remarried, we became U.S. Army dependents in Japan. During those years (the 1950s), I came to appreciate both the American and the Japanese sides of that hyphenate: Japanese-American.

I will connect family stories to each place I travel to with my grandchildren. Like many families, we have generations of stories. Some are in the realm of myth; others are anecdotal. Some are about ghosts. Each story conveys a way of being and experience that enlightens the listener. For example, one day my mother took her garden club to visit a small museum of Japanese art hidden in a labyrinth of houses in Kyoto. When she thought she had found it, she rang the bell and asked to see the treasures. A maid returned with the owner of the house and he regaled them with his collection. "May we have our lunch?" asked my mother. Lunch arrived. At the end of the visit, there was a quiet comment by the owner to my mother that the museum they intended to visit was in the next block.

My four grandchildren are one-quarter Japanese and a combination of other gorgeous inherited traits. If I look closely I see a slight Asian cast to the blue eyes of the youngest. None of the four look related to each other. Each one has carried forward a distinctive characteristic of a family member — a great-grandmother's lips or an auntie's smile. As they grow, I want them to know that my legacy is one wellspring from which they can drink. I have no preset lessons to teach, just the joy of being together in my ancestral home.

61

Grandmother Power

by Paola Gianturco

Paola Gianturco is an author/photographer who has documented women's lives in 55 countries for five books. She has lectured about women's issues in the U.S., Canada, France, and Spain. Her photographs have been exhibited at the UN, the Field Museum, the International Museum of Women, and UNESCO Headquarters in Paris. Gianturco codeveloped and taught Executive Institutes on Women and Leadership at Stanford University, served on the Board of the Association for Women's Rights in Development (AWID), was a principal in the first women-owned advertising agency in the U.S., and is a current member of International Women's Forum.

Seventy candles wouldn't fit on the cake. My grand-girls put a glittery crown on my head instead, and there at the beach, surrounded by bobbing balloons, I became 70.

Then I began my fifth photographic book. I must be the Grandma Moses of photojournalism. My second career started at age 55 after three decades in business, during which I earned millions of frequent-flier miles, which liberated me to work virtually anywhere.

This new book project was compelling and irresistible: I had discovered an unheralded, international activist grandmother movement that was — and is — improving the future for grandchildren everywhere. Assessing our troubled world, grandmothers are saying, "Not good enough for my grandchildren!" and working in groups to make it better.

Grandmother Power: A Global Phenomenon was published by powerHouse Books in 2012. To create it, I went to 15 countries in North and South America, Europe, the Middle East, Africa, and Asia. I interviewed and photographed 120 grandmothers in 17 groups, all fighting for economic, social, and political justice.

Today's grandmothers are an unrecognized resource. They are younger and healthier than grandmothers have ever been. In the northern hemisphere, they are educated and professionally experienced. Many came of age in the 1960s, so they know how to change the world. They're energetic, effective, motivated, and their numbers are growing. Those attributes add up to Grandmother Power.

Some of their work builds on grandmothers' traditional roles:

- African grandmothers are raising grandchildren orphaned by AIDS (100 percent of my author royalties benefit them, via the Stephen Lewis Foundation in Toronto).

- 2,000 Argentine grandmothers are so effective teaching children to love books that the Grandmother Storytelling program has been incorporated into the public school curriculum and copied by eight other countries.

- Members of the Slow Food Movement celebrate International Grandmother's Day every April by teaching their grandchildren to fish, forage, plant, and cook nutritious food, all to curb child obesity.

By contrast, some of their work is inspired by contemporary issues:

- Illiterate, rural Indian grandmothers are learning solar engineering and bringing light to dark villages. Children no longer get lung disease from studying by kerosene lamps; midwives can deliver babies at night; refrigerators now preserve food. The Indian grandmothers are teaching other grandmothers from all over the developing world to be solar engineers.

- Grandmothers in Senegal are convening intergenerational meetings and convincing their villages to stop female genital mutilation, a practice that they had championed and conducted before they learned from community health workers that their daughters were dying in childbirth due to FGM.

Grandmothers aren't just changing the world. By modeling their behavior for younger generations, they are teaching them important values and behaviors, such as collaboration, patience, perseverance, generosity, and resilience.

My dream about *Grandmother Power: A Global Phenomenon,* is that it will inspire grandmothers everywhere to become engaged in the new international grandmothers' movement.

I am convinced it will take all of us, grandMothers and grandOthers, working together, to create hope and possibility for our grandchildren and our world.

62

Learn to See Through the Eyes of Love

by Tina B. Tessina, Ph.D., LMFT

Tina B. Tessina, Ph.D., LMFT, is a licensed psychotherapist in Southern California, with over 30 years' experience in counseling individuals and couples. She is the author of 13 books, which have been translated into 17 languages. Her newest book is *Lovestyles: How to Celebrate Your Differences*. Online, she is "Dr. Romance" with columns at Divorce360 .com, Wellsphere.com, and *Shine* from Yahoo!, and she appears on radio and TV. Tessina publishes *Happiness Tips from Tina*, an e-mail newsletter, and the *Dr. Romance Blog*. She tweets @ tinatessina and is on Facebook at facebook.com/tinatessina and facebook.com/DrRomanceBlog.

When I was about seven, I had a Betsy Wetsy doll that had eyes that closed and the ability to drink a bottle and to wet her diaper (that was major toy technology back in 1949!). After a few years of being left out in the sun and rain, her latex skin was blistered and dirty, and her eyes were rusted.

Grown-ups repeatedly told me to throw her away. But she was my favorite, and I took her everywhere, even on the three-hour family drive to New York City to spend Thanksgiving with my favorite aunt, Ida.

Aunt Ida was a special lady, a laundry seamstress with three children and a loving husband. Even though she was on a very tight budget, as the matriarch of our large Italian family, she always cooked a sumptuous feast for all of us.

At home, after a warm and cozy family weekend in the city, I was dismayed to discover my beloved baby doll was missing, forgotten at Aunt Ida's. Many tears later, I heard my parents call my aunt to verify the doll was there. Ida said she'd keep her safe until our next visit at Christmas. I longed for and worried about the doll, because no one understood how much I loved her.

Finally, at Christmas, again in the city, there was a big box under the tree for me, from Santa. In the box was my doll, looking rather forlorn and as careworn as ever. But she was dressed in a new peach brocade dress, with all the accessories. And there was more . . . carefully wrapped in tissue was a long, white-lace christening dress with a matching hat, slip, and panties, and a lovely gingham puffed-sleeve dress with a lace pinafore and sunbonnet. That poor, battered doll had clothes fit for a princess! Aunt Ida's loving heart and gifted hands had created these exquisite outfits for my doll. It was the most beautiful gift ever! The dresses were magical enough to have come from Santa, but it took an adult who could see through the eyes of a child to understand how important they would be to me.

Many years later, I understood the deeper meaning. To me, my doll represented the parts of myself that were not perfect, and my faults, which were frequently criticized and for which I felt in danger of being rejected. My warm and understanding aunt, a wellspring of maternal love, saw my need and my vulnerability, and showed me in an unforgettable way that even the imperfect parts of myself were deserving of love and attention.

Aunt Ida died when I was 15, and the rest of my family were all gone by the time I was 18. The memory of her love and acceptance has carried me through many hard times since. She truly saw with eyes of love, and you can, too. That's the best gift in the world . . .

63

Gifts Received, Gifts Given

by Roberta Kornfeld Gordon

Whether in a formal classroom setting, meeting, camp, workshop, conference retreat, or convention, Roberta Kornfeld Gordon has been leading and teaching people for 57 years. Her multifaceted career has included helping people of all ages to learn about writing, speaking, and leadership skills in two businesses, WORDPOWER and the School for Writing. These balanced her community efforts, among them working with the Beacon Club, the Darfur Project, and the Breastfeeding Workshop. She lives in Portland, Maine, with her husband, George.

As a child, I loved the joy of receiving a gift, but I couldn't comprehend the giving part . . . why would anyone give anything away to another person? My aunts were abundantly generous in their gift giving to me; yet, while I appreciated their generosity, I couldn't understand how they could give so freely.

In contrast, I couldn't imagine my ever being willing to give a gift to someone. What little I owned was mine, and I wanted to keep everything for myself. Perhaps this stemmed from Mom's Depression-era frugality, which she had instilled in me. She grew up in a loving family in a neighborhood where everyone struggled to make ends meet. That experience impacted her life greatly, and she would implore me to "buy only what you need, so that someday you can buy want you want."

In contrast, Dad was "educated" . . . sent away to schools and camps because of illness in his family. Far from the troubles at home, he immersed himself in learning and music while being welcomed into classmates' homes and lives. Eventually, he married Mom, and together, they created the family life he had missed as a child . . . one filled with songs, stories, and spirit.

Though we didn't have much money, I know now we had riches that money couldn't buy, gifts I wouldn't appreciate until later and that I carry with me today . . . the afghan Mom knitted when I was in seventh grade; the music of our home and family car rides; passages from my bat mitzvah speech; a dedicated Jewish life; and a value system learned from Dad's nightly stories.

My own ability to give changed when I began to babysit. With early earnings, I remember buying two items, a sweater for me and a $1 set of four hospitality plates and cups for my parents. My excitement over giving that gift was a shift for me, a new beginning.

Mothering offered another perspective. My husband, George, and I raised four sons, and now we have daughters-in-law and grandkids as well. The gifts abound. With George as my rock, and the kids teaching, honoring, challenging, and respecting us, we have passed along the treasured life lessons of our past to them, and now we happily watch as they pass on their gifts to the next generation. To give love to one's family and to have it reciprocated surpasses all expectations.

Last year, as I was about to retire from a 30-year position volunteering at the Beacon Club for blind and partially sighted elderly people, I granted three wishes to each member. To name just a few: Debby, a completely blind woman, went (with her transistor radio) to Fenway Park as a VIP to catch all the excitement of a live Red Sox game; Tom, a 95-year-old man, realized his dream to teach a leadership seminar for high school seniors; and Mildred received lunch in the State Dining Room of the Maine governor's residence . . . with a stop-in by the governor! Mildred's end-of-the-day comment spoke for all: "It's not often a 92-year-old person gets her wish granted!"

To that end, I granted one of my own wishes . . . in memory of my sister-in-law, Amelia. On my 70th birthday, I cut 14 inches of my hair to give to Locks of Love, the organization that uses donated tresses to create wigs for young cancer patients.

Yes, over the years, I did learn to give in a way that was meaningful to me. With arms wide open and a full heart, I finally feel at one with my aunts — able to give generously and unconditionally. Today, at age 70, I understand what I could not as a child . . . that the true gift is in the giving.

64

Come to Your Senses

by Patty Cassidy

Patty Cassidy is a horticultural therapist and master gardener who specializes in working with frail elders. She is the president of the Friends of the Portland Memory Garden, one of only two public gardens in the U.S. designed for people living with memory disorders and for their caregivers. Her book, *The Illustrated Practical Guide to Gardening for Seniors*, was published in the fall of 2011 by Anness Press in England, followed by a condensed paperback edition, *The Age-Proof Garden*, from Southwater Books in January 2013. Cassidy currently lives in Portland, Oregon, with her husband, poet and screenwriter Gary Miranda.

The American naturalist John Burroughs once said, "I go to nature to be soothed and healed, and to have my senses put in order." This is sound advice for any age, but especially as we enter our 70s and beyond. And if going "to nature" sounds too grand, then let's just go to a garden and come to our senses!

Smell. "Stop and smell the roses" is also sound advice, but there are plenty of other plants that stimulate our sense of smell. I have a *Daphne odora* in my front rockery that literally stops passersby in their tracks by its fragrance alone. Sweet box near your doorway will have a similar effect. Planting a low-growing aromatic herb like thyme between walking pavers or stones will send wafts of aroma following you on your stroll. Our sense of smell can become less sharp with age, sometimes because of the medications we take. Happily, many different plants can arouse this most nostalgia-inducing sense and bring a flood of memories.

Sight. As we age, our ability to detect certain colors — often pastels and pale hues — is compromised. So the magic word here is "contrast." Think yellow daffodils nodding in front of a dark green hedge, white daisies next to orange crocosmia, or even single flowers with strong contrasts, like black-eyed Susans. Finally, consider the visual kaleidoscope that coleus foliage can offer: contrast, color, and beauty all in one plant.

Sound. This isn't an obvious one, and I'm not about to tell you that bluebells really ring. But many plants do provide their own "music," such as quaking grasses with their whooshing noises, or the percussive clacking of bamboo. Some seedpods also rattle in the wind or when shaken manually. Adding a melodic wind chime or the gentle flow of water are other ways to perk your ears in the garden.

Touch. Fortunately, this sense seems to stay intact no matter what our age. For some of us, getting our hands in the dirt is a satisfying and sensuous experience. Others may prefer feeling plants that are soft and smooth, like lamb's ears or pussy willow. Experiencing the texture of the purple coneflower or succulents such as hens and chicks tells us how diverse and creative Nature can get in her plants. Involve your grandkids. They'll love it!

Taste. For many of us, the diminishment of this sense may be the hardest to accept, but there are ways to renew our tasting ability. For example, using herbs to flavor our food is a healthier option than salt and sugar, and using them fresh from the garden heightens the taste experience. With the caveat "check with your doctor," add edible flowers to salads and desserts for a satisfying taste experience — perhaps peppery-flavored nasturtium flowers, sweet rose petals, or spicy dill flowers.

These are just a few ways to stay in touch — and in smell, sound, taste, and sight — with Nature as we get older. Enjoy!

65

Doing Good and Having Fun

by Peter and Hinda Schnurman

Since 2000, Peter and Hinda Schnurman have volunteered with nongovernmental organizations (NGOs) in the developing world for several months each year, helping to empower people, organizations, and communities. When they are in the U.S., they support and volunteer with nonprofit organizations that also help people fulfill their potential. You can follow their travels and see their photographs at peterandhindas .blogspot.com and peterschnurman.com.

When we lived in Turkey during 1961 and 1962, the president of the country delivered a line in his retirement speech that could be translated as, "When you reach 70, work is finished."

Well, that's not necessarily so for us. We are both over 70, and one of us is still working, at least part-time.

So, what do we do now that we are in our 70s? We work, we volunteer, we travel, and like many our age, we spend time with our families. What we don't do is just sit around waiting for another year to roll by.

About 14 years ago, we began to volunteer in the developing world for three to four months every year. This has given us the opportunity to do the two things we really love: travel and volunteer.

Being in our 70s hasn't really slowed us down. In fact, we think that it energizes us. We may be getting older chronologically, but not in any other way. We believe that staying active by doing the things you love is good for your spirit, and perhaps your physical health as well.

Where have we volunteered? In Thailand, India, Ghana, Uganda, Namibia, Kenya, Mexico, and Ethiopia, and we're currently getting ready to volunteer with a group in northern Tanzania. One of us will be there for only two months because of the need to return to work — and to be close to our six grandchildren; the other will stay for a total of four months.

Overseas, we have volunteered with AIDS organizations, helped to eradicate child labor, raised money, mentored individuals and groups, developed programs and policies, and more important, empowered people and groups, especially women. It is true, at least in a lot of the developing world, that if you empower a woman, you improve the whole village or community.

We saved a young woman from certain death from AIDS in Uganda. In India, we taught a bright woman to use a computer and become an organization director despite her husband's initially thinking that because she was a woman she couldn't learn and do such things. In Kenya, we helped the director of the NGO increase her fundraising skills to such an extent that she was eventually able to raise enough money to build two substantial buildings to house all of the organization's programs so they'd no longer have to pay rent on leased space. We've also developed programs to register and track patients in medical facilities, which helped the clinics to know who they were working with, the number of patients seen each month, etc. And that's just a fraction of all we've done.

Was it hard? Yes! Was it rewarding? Very! Was it fun? Absolutely!

What did we get? We learned how much of the world lives on only a dollar or two a day; we learned a variety of languages and explored different cultures; we discovered new things about ourselves and about each other, despite the fact that we have been married for nearly 53 years. And we have made the world a better place for our children, grandchildren, and lots of others. Recently, on Mother's Day, Hinda received an e-mail from a man we had worked with in Uganda. He wrote: "Many children are enjoying motherly love because your love, courage, and dedicated service gave their parents a new life filled with HOPE." We wake each day to e-mails sent by extended family and friends from all of the countries we've volunteered in, and we smile.

66

Just with Your Heart

by Sally W. Paradysz

Sally W. Paradysz was born, raised, and earned her degree in the Berkshires of New England. Today, she writes her memoirs and fiction in the cabin she built in the woods of her Bucks County, Pennsylvania, home, and it is from there that she pens a weekly blog for those searching for a breath of calm. As an advocate for the self-empowerment of women, she draws upon her own life experiences, bringing the world a message of healing, love, and inspiration. Ordained into the ministry of the Assembly of the Word, founded in Quakertown, Pennsylvania, Paradysz has provided spiritual counseling and ministerial assistance for more than two decades. She is the mother of three and the grandmother of eight, and she's a slave, by choice, to her two flamboyant Maine Coon cats, Kiva and Kodi, who love their life in the woods.

Forests, in any season, are sacred. I have gone to them in reverence for the past seven decades to embrace the smells, tastes, and touch, immersing myself in nature. Soon, the unremarkable becomes remarkable.

Life has challenged me in many ways over these decades, but a walk in the woods lends life force and stability to my existence. I've viewed the struggle in both flora and fauna. Finding strength in this environment empowers me to explore personal values that were previously untapped, and brings me inner peace.

I built a cabin in the woods. I write there, meditate there, and watch the seasons unfold outside my windows. Wild violets, laurel, and ferns are rare and always more precious to me than hothouse flowers. Wetlands nearby are filled with sounds, such as spring peepers or the cry of a heron as he lifts from the reeds. Nature teaches me to live simply and to listen carefully as animals do in order to survive. These lessons have applied to every conversation I've had in my years of spiritual counseling.

The natural world brings me balance, massaging my soul as I curb my needs and experience spiritual joy. In emptiness I find fullness; I thrive by living without distraction. The best place to be is right where you are, finding freedom . . . just with your heart.

When lost or frightened because of sickness or aging, I go to the trees and sit on the leaf-carpeted forest floor.

Leaning against an old oak and feeling the pillow-like softness of the leaves beneath me, I discover much more than the half life I'd been living. My past was filled with attachments and desires that led to disharmony. Taking a deep breath, smelling the richness of the earth, brings back my instinctive balance and teaches me not to overthink or care too little, and to stop to listen to a bird's song, rather than figuring out its source. This subtle education becomes even sweeter as I understand its simplicity.

In interactions with others, I've learned it doesn't matter who is right; to argue is wasted time. It matters more to live within the inherent order of things, appreciating the beauty and harmony inside us. We must be who we are naturally, and not who we want to copy. Age and environment bring wisdom. We can't stop time, but we can embrace the inner quiet that comes with it. Taking moments to enjoy our surroundings allows us to understand time and to feel the power of life that each one of us possesses.

I chose nature and it has healed me. My tension is gone. I feel reassured and assuaged. My fear disappeared when I allowed myself to sit on this earth and feel its vibrations. Surrounding me is the kaleidoscope of seasons — the verdant land bordered by flowering trees and singing birds, the forest in fall with its autumn leaves of gold and red, the snowflakes that whirl toward the frozen earth. All of this exists without judgment.

When I think of others and the choices they have made, "bless them; change me" is the mantra I have learned from nature.

67

Find Your Happy Place (and Get There Already!)

by Sarah-Elizabeth Ratliff

Sarah-Elizabeth Ratliff lives on an organic farm in the interior of Puerto Rico with her husband, Paul, three goats, four dogs, dozens of chickens, and ten farm cats — a life that couldn't be more different from her 25 stressful years in corporate America. As a writer inspired by the cool mountain air and the endless sunshine (broken up by dense tropical rain that brings out the melodic but elusive coquí frog), Ratliff no longer has to complain that "working is getting in the way of what I really want to do in life."

When my husband, Paul, and I were in our early 40s, despite the appearance of having "arrived," we sensed there was something missing from our lives. With two cars in the garage, which was attached to a large suburban home (thanks to excellent salaries, bonuses, and annual stock awards), we wanted for very little. Our friends and family assumed we were happy and fulfilled — and why wouldn't we be? We were both valued in our respective jobs. Paul worked as an information systems administrator, and I was an administrative assistant for a boss who did Very Important Things. We were living the American dream.

Yet we knew that there had to be more to life than being caught up in the all-consuming, consuming-all Southern California lifestyle. We frequently talked about chucking it out the window and becoming self-sustaining organic farmers, because we wanted to give back to Mother Earth, not continue usurping her bountiful gifts.

We visited many locations — Woodstock, New York; the south of France; and southern Maryland — but it was Puerto Rico that called us home. In 2008, our friends and family thought we had taken leave of our senses when we announced we had sold our home, quit our jobs, and given up what many work their whole lives to achieve, so that we could buy a farm. Actually, it was the sanest we had ever been.

Now in our fourth year on the farm, it is obvious that some incredible benefits came from having the guts to reinvent ourselves. Many of those who thought we were crazy now ask us how we did it and if we can help them do the same. We no longer care who won on *American Idol* — we don't even own a TV. A hard day at the office culminates in sweat and a scent that suggests we have been playing with goats, not stressing in endless consternation over office politics. Probably the biggest difference is that we no longer fear the backlash of going against the grain of society to pursue our dreams.

Even at 70 or beyond, it's never too late to reinvent your life. From my experiences, I have learned:

- Life is shockingly short! Don't "wish" your life away!
- If you want to do it, do it!
- Don't do what's expected of you; do what makes you happy!
- Pursue a talent; turn it into something.
- If someone asks your advice, give it; if you need it, ask for it.
- Keep having sex as long as you can!
- Stop caring what people think!
- If you have fractured relationships with loved ones, do your best to fix them, and if they're irreparably broken, move on.

- Don't be fearful — it just makes you stuck.
- Don't be afraid to laugh at yourself!
- Don't spend too much time thinking about the past or the future. Today is what's important.
- If you have pain, don't "oy vey" it away. Go see a doctor or talk with a therapist.
- Be kind and thank people — *often.*
- Take every opportunity to tell the people in your life that you love them.

68

The Keys to Successful Aging . . .

By Carol Orsborn, Ph.D.

Carol Orsborn, Ph.D., is founder of Fierce with Age, the Digest of Boomer Wisdom, Inspiration, and Spirituality. Dr. Orsborn is the best-selling author of 21 books, including her newest publication, Fierce with Age: Chasing God and Squirrels in Brooklyn (Turner Publishing, 2013). She is an internationally known thought leader specializing in issues related to boomer women, spirituality, adult development, and quality of life. She blogs regularly for the Huffington Post, Beliefnet, and NPR's Next Avenue. With a Ph.D. in the history and critical theory of religion from Vanderbilt, she is sought after as a speaker/retreat leader on resilience, aging, and marketing to boomers. Dr. Orsborn, a grandmother, lives in Nashville, Tennessee. She can be reached at carol@fiercewithage.com.

What are two essential things that every 70-year-old needs to know about successful aging?

One: It doesn't "just happen." Those emotionally and spiritually fulfilled octogenarians we hope to someday emulate actually planned for it years earlier.

Two: When it comes to planning for your later years, the most important part is knowing what you can have control over, what you must accept, and as Reinhold Niebuhr put it, "the wisdom to know the difference."

You'll want to remember this the next time you're face-to-face with your financial advisor who asks, "How long do you plan to live?" or "How long will your children be needing financial assistance?" How is it possible to map the years ahead when there are so many variables? The knee-jerk reaction is to go to extremes: conjuring catastrophic scenarios on the one hand or going into denial on the other. The former response will cause you to overreact, the latter will lead you to spin fictions that have nothing to do with the reality of your situation.

Happily, there's an alternative approach that makes it possible for you to plan for a future that is not yours to control. Think about this: by the time we're 70, most of us have already become adept at relying on left-brain thinking to solve problems. But even though we may rely on our rational minds as our first line of defense, we also have the opportunity to develop capacities that we may have underutilized in the past. Neuropsychologists, artists, and mystics all point to untapped reservoirs of intuitive, nonrational insight that, with practice, can increasingly be counted upon to do most of the heavy lifting. Call it "the subconscious," "creativity," or "divine guidance," this alternate way of knowing can bring you clarity far beyond anything your rational mind can deliver.

Ironically, unlike such decisive character traits that we may have relied on in the past — such as will and drive — this alternative approach to planning requires that we surrender our urge to call the shots, and learn to just let go. This is less about "making things happen" and more about receiving and going with the flow.

Here is one technique to get you started. Find a comfortable place where you won't be disturbed for at least a half an hour. Make sure you have some paper and a pen. At the top of the page, write: "What would I like to do in my life, now that I've reached my 70s?" For the next 30 minutes, write nonstop whatever comes into your mind. Don't "lead" your thoughts. Rather, follow them, as if taking dictation. The only rule is that you refrain from judging or censoring your train of thought.

After a while, many people report that a voice of wisdom kicks in, tapping inner resources in unexpected ways. Suddenly, where there was confusion and indecision, there is certainty. Even if you don't get an answer on your first effort, know that you are giving your subconscious mind permission to play a bigger role in your life.

The truth is, you can't know for sure what the future may bring. But the deeper you dig inside yourself, the more you'll be able to tap your personal intuition, which will help you navigate whatever path your life may take.

69

The View (Downfield) from 70

by Ronald J. Manheimer, Ph.D.

Ronald J. Manheimer, Ph.D., is the former founding director of the North Carolina Center for Creative Retirement, a lifelong learning, leadership, community service, and research institute at the University of North Carolina–Asheville, where he was also research associate professor of philosophy. He is the author of A Map to the End of Time: Wayfarings with Friends and Philosophers, Older Americans Almanac, The Second Middle Age, and other publications on aging, philosophy, and human development. In partial retirement, Manheimer is learning how to take some of the advice he's given to others. His Web site is at ronmanheimer.com.

"Hey, Levi. Throw it, buddy," I shout to my grandson who is standing across the grassy field, tossing his new football in the air. Levi, tall and gangly for an 11-year-old, looks up, nods, and trots back maybe 20 yards. He cocks his arm and fires off a beautiful spiral. I dance backward a few steps before I realize the ball is going to sail right over my head. I take off running, looking over my shoulder in hopes that I can preserve my grandfatherly pride and snag the ball. My heart pounding, I hear the roar of an invisible crowd.

I first started taking Levi for outings on Wednesdays after school when he was 7 and I was 66. At the time, we started out with a Frisbee. Teaching him the knack of throwing it sent me running hither and yon to catch up with the wildly curving disk. Then, one day, he made the saucer glide straight through my fumbling fingers and into my gut. Levi laughed. Gradually, Levi's two younger brothers, Greyson, now eight, and Asa, five, joined us. Together, we go bowling, play miniature golf, visit museums (art, mineral, science), hike through the local bird sanctuary, and watch the antics of the river otters at the nature center. Every outing culminates at one of our area ice cream stores.

Because I want to keep up with understanding their evolving ways of perceiving the world around them, I avoid passive activities like going to the movies or to one of those indoor game places the boys sometimes get invited to for birthday parties. I want our time together to be fun and active, but also to give us a way to hang out and talk about how our lives are coming along.

Each boy is different. You can't really ask Levi direct questions. He just decides when he's got something to talk about and when he doesn't. Sometimes, after a long period of relative silence on a trail or in the halls of a museum, he'll just reach over and take my hand. That's it. Greyson, by contrast, has much to say about the goings on among his friends, school field trips, neighborhood pets, and speculations on how gravity works in empty space. For Asa, who loves to draw pictures of houses and build them out of wooden blocks, the whole world is the subject of fantasies in which he may play the role of a giant, a mouse, an alien, or an architect.

As the boys master the handling of disks, bowling balls, bats, and putters, and the mental skills of reading, calculating, and theorizing, their grandfather partly relives his youth, partly marvels at the amazing energy and enthusiasm of childhood, and partly takes note that, as they develop, he ages. *Wistful* and *grateful* are the two words that bracket the span of my emotions.

Back to me running and reaching skyward — yes, I do get one hand on the ball and pull it in. *Wow,* I'm thinking, *that kid can really throw.* I turn and look at Levi in the distance. He gives me an approving thumbs-up. Then it hits me: how am I going to throw the football all the way back to him? I wave to the crowd, run forward, and let fly.

70

Lessons from the Amulet Maker

by Kendall Dudley, M.A.

Kendall Dudley, M.A., directs Lifeworks Career and Life Design in Arlington, Massachusetts, through which he leads multimedia life-story programs, retreats, and intentional-travel trips abroad. He's taught at Tufts and Lesley universities, consulted to Harvard for 15 years, and presents on creativity and life direction at national conferences. His public art and social-justice projects have received support from the Massachusetts Cultural Council, among others. He is program chair for the Life Planning Network's New England chapter and a contributor to their book *Live Smart After 50!* Dudley has degrees from the Wharton School and Columbia, and he was in the Peace Corps in Iran. Visit his Web site at kendalldudley.com.

I began turning 70 last year in the Djmaa-al-Fna, the overwrought yet magical center of Marrakech. There I met an amulet maker who occupies a carpet in the vast market space he shares with acrobats, storytellers, musicians, and trance healers. Sitting like a nomadic king in yellow robes, he asked what form of protection I wanted. I said health for myself, my family, and my friends . . . and peace for the world. He paused for a moment and then took out his collection of brass amulets, chose one, and set about selecting its contents.

From a tray of many elements, he broke off a piece of bird wing and wedged it into the core of the brass cylinder to which he added ginger, silver, salt, and myrrh. From a small box under his knee, he chose a pinch of crushed blue stone. Carefully, he seated each ingredient into the amulet, twisted the top closed and presented it to me in his open palm. It shone in his copper hand. I thanked him, and he gave a slight bow as though offering a blessing. I returned his bow and, in that moment, felt a spark between us.

I walked on, but the encounter stayed fixed within me. How could I begin to understand what had happened? The amulet maker drew on folk beliefs and traditional notions of healing and the power of nature's elements to "protect" me. Perhaps he was a charlatan; perhaps not. Instead of dismissing him, I chose to see him as part of a wider world I knew little to nothing about. I am trained to disregard such ideas — but here, surrounded by a culture infused with the West but resolutely clinging to tradition, I chose to listen.

Turning 70, I feel I'm in no place to dismiss sources of new knowledge, for I am learning how little I know about life outside the zone defined by my class, education, and the sway of friends. I am in a box of my own construction, largely aided in its design by the culture around me. That culture keeps me rewarded and comfortable, but at what cost? If comfort robs me of the zeal to explore the unknown aspects of myself, it serves little purpose. If the gift of age invites me to rest on my laurels, it will not awaken me to the circumstances and suffering of others and the need to offer some kind of relief.

The amulet maker awakens me to listen to what is beckoning me, even if it is not in a form I readily recognize.

At 70, time clears the table before me. It sweeps away clutter and lets me see essences. Time tells me that writing, painting, teaching, and traveling are vital. It tells me that family, friends, and my ever-expanding community are central. But it does not tell me how to wrap all these together. So, lest my fuel supplies get spent on glittery surfaces, habit, and propriety, I'm paying close attention, even to the signs and symbols contained within an amulet. For they may offer routes into a future I could not find using only the contents of my box.

About the Commissioning Editor

Mark Evan Chimsky is editor in chief of the book division of Sellers Publishing, an independent publishing company based in South Portland, Maine. For eight years, he ran his own editorial consulting business. Previously he was executive editor and editorial director of Harper San Francisco and headed the paperback divisions at Little, Brown and Macmillan. In addition, he was on the faculty of New York University's Center for Publishing, and for three years he served as the director of the book section of NYU's Summer Publishing Institute. He has edited a number of best-selling books, including Johnny Cash's memoir, *Cash*, and he has worked with such notable authors as Melody Beattie, Arthur Hertzberg, Beryl Bender Birch, and Robert Coles. He was also project manager on Billy Graham's *New York Times* best-selling memoir, *Just As I Am*. He conceived of the long-running series *The Best American Erotica*, which was compiled by Susie Bright, and he was the first editor to reissue the works of celebrated novelist Dawn Powell. His editorial achievements have been noted in *Vanity Fair*, the *Nation*, and *Publishers Weekly*. He is an award-winning poet whose poetry and essays have appeared in *JAMA* (the *Journal of the American Medical Association*), *Wild Violet*, *Three Rivers Poetry Journal*, and *Mississippi Review*. For Sellers Publishing, he has developed and compiled a number of books, including *Creating a Life You'll Love*, which won the silver in *ForeWord's* 2009 Book of the Year Awards (self-help category), *65 Things to Do When You Retire*, which *The Wall Street Journal* called "[one] of the year's best guides to later life," and *65 Things to Do When You Retire: Travel*.

About the Associate Project Editor

Renee Rooks Cooley is a freelance editor and proofreader based in South Portland, Maine. She is a *summa cum laude* graduate and valedictorian of Emerson College, where she received a B.F.A. in creative writing. A former staff proofreader for Houghton Mifflin's school division, Renee began her publishing career as a longtime poetry screener and office manager for *Ploughshares* magazine. Her poetry has appeared in literary publications, including the *Washington Square Review*. She was the associate project editor for *65 Things to Do When You Retire*, published by Sellers Publishing.

Credits